THE OTHER SIDE OF MIND

A Journey through Bipolar Disorder

SARAH SMYTH

iUniverse, Inc.
Bloomington

The Other Side of Mind
A Journey through Bipolar Disorder

iUniverse books may be ordered through booksellers or by contacting:

iUniverse
1663 Liberty Drive
Bloomington, IN 47403
www.iuniverse.com
1-800-Authors (1-800-288-4677)

ISBN: 978-1-4502-8317-5 (sc)
ISBN: 978-1-4502-8318-2 (ebook)

Printed in the United States of America

iUniverse rev. date: 1/31/2011

TABLE OF CONTENTS

Introduction   xi

1. Descent into Hell   1
2. A Home Away from Home   17
3. A Bit of History   43
4. Diagnosis   70
5. Outcomes of Bipolar Disorder   108
6. The Treatment of Bipolar Disorder   130
7. Other Issues   146
8. Survive and Thrive   172

Afterword   185

Bibliography   189

ACKNOWLEDGMENTS

It is with much gratitude that I thank the many people who supported me during my illness and in the writing of this book: to David Chilton for his encouragement and expertise in marketing strategies, to my mother, Pat Smyth and my aunt Ellie Smyth who always wondered when this book would finally be finished, to my dear friend Cathy Falconer who has always been there for me, to my friend Michelle Kritzinger for her advice and support, to Jasmine Wang for her enthusiasm, ideas and assistance and for putting up with me when I was ill, to Michael Holker for support in helping me organize the text and tell my story with compassion for the reader, to Dr. V. Raghu-Raman for keeping me on track and healthy, to Gloria Olsen for her friendship and support, to my brother Josh for his encouragement, to the patients I met who inspired me to write this book, and to my late father, Hugh Smyth who always believed in me.

In memory of my father

INTRODUCTION

What does it feel like to lose your mind? Never in my wildest dreams did I ever think that I would have an answer to that question, but I do now.

I suffer from Bipolar Disorder and have experienced devastating depressions and severe manias which were so highly disturbing, I never thought I would ever recover. In the past, I nearly lost the will to live and then in contrast, at other times felt that it was my job to save the world. Gripped by psychosis, I have had episodes of depression and mania where I completely lost touch with reality and experienced frightening hallucinations and delusions.

There have been times during this illness when I thought I would lose everything permanently – my family, my friends, my job, my home and my money. During my last episode of mania my life was in such ruins that I became perilously close to living on the street.

Miraculously, in 2006 I was given one more chance to beat bipolar disorder and my story will take you on a journey through the catastrophic depths of this illness, into despair and madness and finally toward recovery and wellness once again.

Could I have stopped all this from happening in the first place? Probably not. Although, we presently have an ever increasing grasp of knowledge about bipolar disorder, there is still a great deal we don't know. For years, my doctors and I simply didn't have the answers.

The symptoms of bipolar disorder are exaggerated versions of the feelings of sadness and happiness. Thoughts and feelings are extremely altered and patients experience extremely disrupted sleep and energy levels. Behaviour may become bizarre and dangerous and severe illness may lead to suicide. Bipolar disorder is not a trifling matter.

It is my purpose in this book to share my experiences which include my journey into and through the illness as well as the road to recovery which I am on now.

My story begins with a whirlwind tour of psychotic mania and the experiences and feelings I dealt with in that state. Chapter 2 reveals some family history and sheds light on even earlier episodes of depression and mania that I experienced. In chapter 3, I will navigate through the diagnostic process while chapter 4 discusses a variety of possible outcomes of bipolar disorder. An in-depth investigation of treatment I underwent is the subject of chapter 5 while chapter 6 explores other issues such as sleep, creativity, identity and bipolar disorder in children and youth. Finally, chapter 7 reveals my experience of a bumpy but rewarding journey into recovery, hope and wellness.

Although all of the characters in this book are real, I have changed the names of patients and doctors in order to maintain confidentiality.

CHAPTER 1
DESCENT INTO HELL

Into an oversized pink handbag I stuffed one thing after another: bottles of perfume, deftly removed from their boxes, cosmetics, soaps and lotions. I kept talking to myself, coaching myself to steal as much as I could fit into my bag. There was no-one around, so I had every advantage. Suddenly however, I noticed a girl with long blonde hair on a ladder to my right. She was laughing at me and telling me that I was stupid. I got back to business and cleared the shelves of merchandise, sneaking articles out of their packages and carefully placing the empty wrappings and boxes back on the shelves. Then all at once, the girl on the ladder vanished.

My heart began to race. I knew that I was shoplifting but felt out of control. I couldn't even recall how I got into the store or what time of day it was. Completely oblivious to my surroundings, I continued to steal.

Suddenly I stopped what I was doing and looked up. There was no-one to be seen. Frozen , I wondered, "What do I do now"? I looked at my watch and it read 10:15 p.m. The store had actually been closed for the last 45 minutes. The girl on the ladder must have been a hallucination. With that realization, I started to panic and became very confused. I was the only person left in this grocery store. "Nobody has seen me," I thought. I made a run for it. Dashing down the stairs with my handbag full of loot, my heart racing and my head spinning like a top, I made for the exit, tense but feeling victorious.

As I took my first step out the door, I heard heavy footsteps coming up behind me. Before I knew what was happening, someone grabbed my arm and two other men appeared in front of me. "Oh, God", I thought. "I've been caught!" I froze on the spot. Then out of nowhere approached seven or eight security guards. The one who had my arm alerted me that I was under arrest for shoplifting and instructed me to put my handbag down on the floor. I did so, but then immediately began to panic. Sobbing, I told the security guards that I didn't mean to steal and truly, I didn't really comprehend what I had done. "Save your tears for the police", one of them retorted. "We've dealt with people like you for a long time". When I turned around I witnessed a group of men in black security uniforms staring coldly at me. In shock, I began shaking and my knees buckled as I fell to the floor. The guard who had a grip on my arm yanked me up and escorted me to the ground floor security office in the store. One of the other men retrieved my handbag from the floor and brought it along. I began to cry uncontrollably, begging the guards not to call the police, but it was too late.

I was instructed to sit down in a cold, metal chair. The contents of my handbag were dumped out onto a table in front of me and everyone, including me, was astounded by the amount of merchandise I had stockpiled into my bag. One of the men then produced a large box into which he placed all the items except my wallet which was left on the table.

"Please don't send me to jail", I sobbed. "I'm sick. I'll pay for everything". "Oh, stop your blubbering", the rude guard yelled. "We deal with people like you all the time. You're a real pro at this, aren't you?" "No I'm not so please stop speaking to me like that", I pleaded. "You took a lot of loot, lady, so how did you think you were going to get away with this?" another guard questioned. "There's something wrong with me", I gasped. "I will go to the hospital first thing tomorrow morning". "Didn't you see us right beside you while you were taking all that stuff?" another guard asked me. "No. I only saw a girl on a ladder", I replied, "and she was talking about me". "This one's fucking nuts"! the rude guard interrupted.

Then the police arrived – two officers. One was diplomatic, the other more abrupt. I began to panic again and felt my heart racing and my chest pounding with pain. The officers first took a report from the security guards then asked me to explain my side of the story. I was hyperventilating by this time, worried that I was going to jail. The kinder officer advised me that I was being arrested and charged but since I was not a repeat offender, I would not presently go to jail. I was then able to take a few deep breaths but the chest pain persisted.

After questioning, the police explained to me what would happen and made me sign a bunch of papers but I didn't really comprehend any of this, except for the fact that I would have to appear in court. The police informed me that I had stolen nearly a thousand dollars worth of merchandise and that I would have to pay for it all plus damages. I kept reiterating that I would be calling an ambulance to take me to the hospital in the morning.

After much questioning, the police handed me a yellow slip of paper which I lost within hours. Apparently, that paper stated all the terms and conditions of the charges including the fact that I would not be allowed to return to the store for one year. I was trying to calm down but I couldn't make sense of what they were saying. Desperately trying to control my disorganized thoughts, I managed to blurt out that I would never steal again, then started to cry once more.

After about two hours, the police were finished with me and somehow I had the audacity to ask for a ride home as it was well past midnight and buses had stopped running in the area.

The following morning, I woke up terrified and confused and called an ambulance. It was clear that I needed psychiatric help but I didn't know what was wrong with me. Paranoid, I was escorted out of my apartment and taken to the local hospital where I was isolated in a crisis room, awaiting an assessment by the psychiatric crisis team. I was not allowed to leave the room and was watched by a security guard. While staring at the walls across from me, it appeared as if there was a television screen in front of me and on it I saw violent pictures depicting people being tortured and killed. When I looked away then returned my gaze the pictures were gone. However, I thought I heard the security guard telling me that I was stupid to stay in the hospital. I must have been hallucinating because no sound could be heard behind the door to the crisis room.

After several hours had passed, the psychiatric team of doctors and nurses came to assess me and deemed me well enough to go home. Against my wishes I was released and told to increase the dosage of a medication called Seroquel, which, although it works for many people, wasn't working for me. I left the hospital bewildered and upset and was afraid to go home. There was no money in my wallet or bank account so I was given taxi fare by one of the crisis nurses.

Once home my anxiety continued to mount as a got out of the car and approached the door to my apartment building. I was afraid to go in, thinking an intruder was inside. At that point, I turned on my heels, ran out the door and got on a bus to God knows where. Somehow I ended up in the far west end of Toronto at a financial outlet which provides loans to just about anybody with a 35 percent interest rate. I borrowed three thousand dollars and spent the entire amount at a vintage clothing store in the middle of nowhere and went home penniless again.

I don't recall how I got home, but I did enter my apartment this time even though I was hearing noises and voices. Unable to sleep, I remained highly alert throughout the night, and thus turned on my stereo to block out the noise in my head. However, I must have dozed off for a short time because when I opened my eyes, I saw that it was morning. For some reason I arose with a searing pain in my right leg and the sensation that my right foot was frozen. I wondered if this was all in my head – if I was having another hallucination, and yet the pain was very real. In addition, my heart began to pound and I knew that I was heading towards another panic attack and thought that I must get back to the hospital and into psychiatric care as soon as possible. Clearly, my medication wasn't working. I called the ambulance again.

Because of the pain in my leg however, I was admitted directly to the cardiac unit when I got to the hospital. Feeling paranoid, I kept asking the paramedics if I was going to die. The pain in my leg was excruciating and it became necessary to medicate me with Demerol from an intravenous drip. Although I received a large dose, I experienced only minimal relief and spent the night awake once again. Doctors were unable to diagnose anything wrong with me (yet a few months later I was admitted again for blood clots in both lungs and this may have been related).

Still feeling the pain in my leg, I addressed my psychiatric concerns with one of the doctors but was sent home again following yet another adjustment to the same medication I was already taking. As I left the hospital, I heard everyone waiting in the emergency area laughing at me and calling me names, but even though I told myself that this was just another hallucination, I yelled at the patients before walking out of the building.

It was now Thursday morning and I was given taxi fare yet again in order to get home. Upon entering the driver's car I heard a news broadcast on the radio about the status of my mental health. The radio host was warning people about me and telling people how crazy I was. Horrified, I asked the driver if the man on the radio was referring to me. He replied by telling me that the radio wasn't even on. However, I continued to hear commentary about me from the dispatch officer and other drivers calling in to make fun of me. My driver asked me to sit quietly, which I did. I was at this time heading into psychosis and the voices on the radio were in fact auditory hallucinations.

I managed to arrive home safely without saying anything else in the car and entered my building only to witness a young couple in the lobby making fun of me, laughing and sneering in my direction. "I must have been talking to myself", I thought, and looked down in embarrassment. When I glanced up again, the couple had vanished. In the hallway, the superintendent asked me who I had been talking to. He informed me that nobody but me was present. Frightened by this knowledge, I kept my head down and ran to the elevator.

When I stepped out on my floor, I encountered a man and a woman standing on a wooden ladder in my hallway, and it appeared as though they were making repairs to the wall. The woman was blonde and looked like the same person I had seen in the grocery store during my shoplifting nightmare. I walked around the couple and heard the woman whisper things about me to her partner. I rushed to open the door of my apartment, got inside then slammed the door shut. I must have had yet another hallucination. In order to verify this, I immediately looked out into the hallway and saw, of course, that nobody was there. By this time I knew that my hallucinations had become visual and auditory and that realization scared the daylights out of me.

At this point in time, I was trying to control panic attacks, get a grip on reality and get help. I ran to my bedroom to call my friend Cathy at her place of work. In serious trouble, I was experiencing a barrage of distorted sensations and perceptions, and because I was cognizant of the fact that I was having hallucinations, I asked Cathy if she was real. I then cried that I was afraid I might do something dangerous to hurt myself or that I might die from my symptoms. Someone at Cathy's end of the line, a colleague perhaps, managed to call the police and an ambulance while Cathy remained on the phone with me. Paramedics arrived at my address while I was still on the phone, but I was bewildered and unable to get myself organized to get out the door and go to the hospital. Then the police arrived, but severe cognitive disorganization and paranoia made me think that they were evil people in disguise. When they first entered my apartment, I ran back into my bedroom and slammed the door shut behind me. I heard the officers poking fun at me on the other side of the door (another auditory hallucination).

However, with police accompaniment the ambulance took me back to the emergency ward of the same hospital, yet again. I was becoming suicidal and threatened to slash my wrist if I was sent home again. As a result, I was guarded by police and security guards after being placed in the crisis room. I asked the police to stay in the room with me because I thought, if I was left alone, I would find a way to kill myself. As a result of my hallucinations, I had to ask the police not to talk about me as if I wasn't there.

Six hours passed before the crisis team came to see me that time. In short, they assigned another doctor to my case who said that I had a behaviour disorder and a bad attitude yet I was too shocked to argue with him. He gave me yet another prescription and sent me on my way.

While I was waiting in the hospital pharmacy for my prescription to be filled, a man shuffled in, addressed me by name and called me the "brown-eyed girl". He had wild protruding eyes, dark, dishevelled hair, a slight build and an unkempt appearance, and yet he seemed to know what was wrong with me and advised me (among other things) that he was my guardian angel. I informed him that I was going to be giving a lecture on psychosis for all physicians at the hospital on the following morning.

Several minutes later, while I was still talking to the man, the pharmacist came over to me and escorted me to a chair. He informed me that no-one was in the pharmacy except for me and that I was talking to someone who wasn't there. I immediately covered my eyes and put my head down. A brief moment later, when I lifted my head, sure enough, no-one was in the pharmacy except me and the pharmacist. He insisted that I take a dosage of the new medication (I don't remember what it was) before leaving his store. By this time, I was so cognitively disorganized that I lost the prescription before I got home and never found out its name.

For the second time that Thursday, I took a cab home (obviously paid for by the hospital). When I walked into my apartment I saw a secret code on the wall across from me and thought it had special meaning and that I must figure it out. Suddenly I felt totally connected with the universe. The code made sense and everything around me felt meaningful. Grabbing one of my journals, I started to write down ideas and concepts, and developed theories and formulas about how these concepts were related. I felt omnipotent and brilliant, like I'd just had a stroke of genius. I came up with titles for books and plays- hundreds of them. My pen wouldn't stop. In the middle of the night, I called my mother to tell her the good news. I had somehow, miraculously healed myself! The worst was over, or so I thought. Needless to say, I was actually in the crux of a psychotic manic episode and these wild symptoms were but another indicator. That night, I slept for about one hour on the couch, then tried to go to sleep in my bed but rest eluded me yet again.

Friday morning came and I was out of my mind. Sobbing uncontrollably, I took the bus to the hospital. I felt completely alone. This time the emergency psychiatrist sent me upstairs to register for the mental health day treatment program but I just sat outside the nurses' station and sobbed for hours. When a nurse finally addressed me and asked me if I was finished crying, I conveyed to her that I had just about given up hope. For four days in a row I had attempted to get admitted into psychiatric care and for those same four days, I had been released from emergency and sent home.

My memory of the next 24 hours is weak. I have tried since to solicit information from others about what happened to me but apparently, I did not contact anyone during that time. Saturday night however, would be a night I would never forget.

By evening, I was convinced that I was possessed by the devil (a delusion) and would never sleep again. Thoughts of a dreadful death consumed me, such as being set on fire, having all my skin peeled off and being cut up with thousands of knives. Again I paced between bedroom and living room trying to find a safe place to sleep. I turned on the television to block out the noises and voices around me then witnessed messages on the TV screen telling me that I was going to die. These messages were written at the bottom of the screen in bold red letters. Next, I saw an image on the screen that I will never forget. It may not seem like much to the reader but it convinced me that I was possessed. On the left side, I saw a panel in red. Then an old car appeared with horns extending out of its sides. Next I detected a hawk diving out of the sky towards the car, smashing into it and causing a huge explosion. I was petrified by this image and by the haunting cry of the hawk so immediately, I changed the channel. Once again, beneath the picture, I saw messages telling me to beware of the devil and to stay awake all night in order to avoid being snatched away by it.

I was completely out of touch with reality at that point and was very frightened by the images I saw on the television. Shutting it off, I ran back to my bedroom. I turned on all the lights, but didn't feel like I was in my own home. Bombarded by voices and noises, I held my head, curled up into a ball on top of my bed and rocked back and forth to try blocking out the stimuli.

Thus began the final episode of terror, my descent into hell, I surmised. I prayed for God to help me, spoke for hours to crisis nurses on the phone and completely lost the ability to cope. Sleep, of course, was impossible. Somehow, I acquired the idea that I must not sleep before six a.m. or I would permanently enter into hell under the orders of the devil. In my state, I had no trouble staying awake past this time and thought therefore that I had been freed of the devil's influence and certain death. However, after I got out of bed, walked to the kitchen and looked out the window, I heard the cry of a large bird and saw "the raven", Edgar Allen Poe's bird of death. Again, terribly alarmed, I thought I was going to die. At seven a.m. I called my friend Cathy and told her that I had lost my mind. Whatever else she said, (I can't recall all of it), she advised me to get dressed and get to church for the early service. I immediately followed her instructions, threw on some clothes and fled my apartment on foot, in the direction of my church.

It was mid November. Dressed in a T-shirt and jeans, I literally ran the two kilometres to church that morning. An eerie feeling of unreality surrounded me as I sped down the street and I felt like I was hundreds of years in the past. It was as if I had been looking through the lens of a camera as an observer of the world, not a participant. I even wondered if I was dead. As I got closer to my church, I accelerated my pace, still hearing the hollow, deadly cry of the raven above me.

Finally I reached the church and gasping for air, I pulled open the heavy wooden door at the entrance. Immediately, I experienced another hallucination. Suddenly, I detected the sounds of bells and choral Christmas music above me, and the laughter of Santa Claus. Turning in the direction of the clamour, I noticed two televisions fixed at the top of the double entrance doors. As I looked up, I saw images of angels, Christmas trees, Santa and bells in vivid colour. When I averted my gaze and looked back again, the two televisions had disappeared and I realized that I'd had yet another hallucination.

Exhausted and out of breath, I approached a man who was greeting parishioners as they came in. With effort, holding back tears, I informed him that I was having a "spiritual crisis". For some reason, that was the first thing that came out of my mouth. Next, I asked him if I was dead. He assured me that I was not, reached into his pocket for his cell phone and summoned the parish nurse. He then seated me against a wall in the main lobby of the sanctuary. According to the greeter, I was apparently quite incoherent and was asked to sit quietly while the rest of the congregation filed in. No-one looked at me so I thought I was invisible, perhaps a ghost. Within a few minutes, the nurse arrived and thought that I was having a panic attack and a psychotic break. Convinced of my mortality, I asked her if I was dead and she replied that I was not, but she wanted me to go to the hospital. Fortunately, the nurse found a kind member of the congregation to drive me to the emergency ward. Coraline introduced herself, and reassured me that I was not going to die, but nevertheless informed me that we all die eventually. I would have been more comfortable if she had just left that out! Coraline held my hand as we departed from the church premises in her car.

During the drive to the hospital, the surroundings once again seemed unreal. I was completely disoriented with respect to space and time and felt like I had gone back into the past.

Once we reached the hospital, I pleaded with Coraline to come into the emergency ward with me and not to leave me alone. I was petrified by my state of mind and by the possibility that I might get sent home yet again without appropriate treatment. After having registered with the triage nurse, we were guided to a crisis room. Unable to make light conversation, I spoke to Coraline about life and death and what it was like to be half way in between (or so I thought). I also told her that I could communicate with dead spirits and that I could see things that she couldn't. I was without a doubt completely delusional at that point. Coraline attempted to pray for me but it didn't help.

After about an hour, we were asked to move to the regular emergency waiting room and to listen for my name. Suddenly I had a feeling (a delusion actually) that I had been sent a message from God about what was happening here. God was giving me a preview of death. All of my hallucinations were trying to tell me something – that this was my judgement day and if I didn't "pass", I would be killed and sent to hell.

Poor Coraline tried to talk some sense into me but I would have none of it. Instead, I advised her that this trip to the hospital was very serious, that I was being given a chance to turn my life around and would have to prove myself to God. I was having another delusional religious experience. Even though I knew I was ill on one level, I felt that there was some sort of divine purpose for my being here in the hospital. I thought that the doors to the emergency ward were actually the gates to heaven or hell; I didn't know which. I wondered what would happen to me on the other side.

Suddenly my name was called. "Oh, no"! I gasped. Coraline assured me that I would be safe. Slowly I got up and walked toward the doors and the triage nurse who I thought was the "gatekeeper". At the double doors I hesitated, but the "gatekeeper" told me that I was going to a safe place. Coraline finally got to let go of my hand and I heard the emergency doors close solidly behind me. I was in – on the "other side". "Are you real"? I asked a kind woman who addressed me and asked me a few simple questions. "Are you an angel"? I wondered out loud. The young nurse was congenial. She didn't try to talk me out of my delusions or hallucinations. After responding to her questions, I asked her if I passed the test. She went along with me and said yes, and added that a room was being prepared for me.

I made it! Thank God. I was not going to hell. After a week of attempts to get admitted to the hospital, I was finally accepted as a psychiatric in-patient. However, my delusional self was doing the reasoning at that point. I realized that I was not in hell. An immediate rush of relaxation flowed over me and I told the nurse that I was "delighted" to be there. I felt a bit like Ebenezer Scrooge in Dickens' "A Christmas Carol" when he realizes that he hasn't missed Christmas — that the spirits have done it all in one night.

Placed in a wheelchair, I was taken down a long, stretcher-lined hallway toward the elevator. Suddenly, en route, I bolted out of the chair, overwhelmed by the sight of vivid colours in my surroundings and intense medicinal aromas. I expressed my surprise to the nurse who insisted that I sit down again. I must have blacked out momentarily because the next thing I can recall is that I was being woken up by another benevolent nurse who giggled and wheeled me into a bright cafeteria.

CHAPTER 2
A HOME AWAY FROM HOME

Seven West was the name of the locked psychiatric ward where I found myself for the second time that year, but I didn't recognize a thing. Still slipping in and out of reality, I had the sense that I was here, then there, then somewhere else – a disjointed feeling of bouncing from one place to the next within the few minutes I had been on the ward. I don't remember transitions (for example, walking between rooms), just various endpoints.

Then while I was in the cafeteria awaiting the preparation of my room, I noticed another woman in a wheelchair, both legs outstretched in front of her in full casts from toe to hip. I could see that she was tall and that she was very uncomfortable in her predicament. She said hello and I reciprocated. I asked what happened to her, pointing to the casts and she replied that she had broken both heels and did not want to discuss her condition any further. She asked why I was in the ward. I explained that I was having a spiritual crisis and that God let me in, had forgiven me for my sins and was preparing me to enter Heaven. The nurses and doctors were going to help me get there. On one level, I knew that I had bipolar disorder but the illness seemed to me at the time to be a symptom of my "spiritual crisis", not an illness in its own right.

Elaine, baffled by my response, wheeled herself closer to me and I noticed that she had several fingers missing from both hands. I didn't ask her about that. Kindly, she offered to play me a game of cards later on and I accepted. She had a pleasant enough appearance but something wasn't right about her countenance. Her eyes bulged out from her face and gave me the impression that she was on the alert, and was preparing for an emergency. She had short brown, rather dirty hair, a soiled hospital gown, and overall, she appeared quite dishevelled. I suspected that she may have attempted suicide by jumping off something (quite rightly as I found out later). Elaine's private room had a one-way glass window in it, for observation. I wondered if she was still as risk for suicide and if she had cut off her own fingers, but I never found out. Nevertheless, Elaine presented herself as calm and cheerful. After confirming our plans for later, she wheeled herself out of the cafeteria and I was left by myself for a short time.

Within a few moments, another patient, a man, entered, dressed completely in white from head to toe. At first I thought he was an employee of the hospital since he was clean, well-groomed and fit. He said his name was Joseph and I, believing in the religious significance of everything, including his name, replied, "Of course it is". In tune with my delusions he asked me if I was Mary and although I said no, replied that I knew why he asked. For a few minutes we talked about God and Jesus and both of us felt that we had been sent here (to Seven West) to fulfill a special purpose. I advised Joseph that I would explain his mission to him later, once I got settled. He communicated an eagerness to hear about this mission and confirmed that he would meet me at the dinner hour. I assumed that Joseph (actually, that was his last name) was a holy person since he was wearing all white and was so clean and neat. "Cleanliness is next to Godliness", I announced as he left the cafeteria.

Looking around, I began to take notice of my surroundings. The cafeteria was stark, with beige walls, a gray linoleum floor and a sink with cupboards above it at one end of the room. There were no pictures or decorations but there was a television mounted at the top of the wall at the opposite end. Well worn wooden tables rested on the floor and plastic, classroom-styled chairs were tucked in at each table. The room looked like it would seat about thirty people and I suspected that all meals were taken here. Bright fluorescent lights contributed to the clinical atmosphere of the room and it seemed a bit unwelcoming.

A few moments later, my nurse entered and confirmed that my room was ready. I had nothing to carry but my purse as I'd come to the emergency ward directly from church. The nurse escorted me down the hallway and as I passed another patient's room, I heard yelling, banging and swearing coming from within.

There were three security guards standing outside the door. For some reason, I was not alarmed and told the security guards, "He will be healed soon enough". Two doors down from his room, I was introduced to mine, a double, not a ward. I was relieved. After escorting me to my side of the room, my nurse told me to put on a hospital gown and to lock up my clothes in the closet provided.

Looking at the bed beside me, I beheld a young woman who looked, well, mentally ill. She was emaciated, with sunken eyes, a pale complexion and greyish teeth. She was lying on her bed, a tangled mop of thin greasy hair spread out on her pillow. As the nurse was giving me instructions, my roommate woke up and we introduced ourselves to each other. She indicated that her name was Jennifer and that she was a saved Christian. I was eager to hear more from her. Jennifer informed me that I had been sent from God to help her get well. We were sharing delusions at that point and I believed her at once. She was indeed, as it turned out, schizophrenic. Convinced that my hospital experience was a religious one, I sat on my bed momentarily and looked out my window then began to laugh hysterically. I witnessed an enormous neon blue "H" (which of course stands for "Hospital") up to my left, one floor above. Jubilantly, I shrieked to Jennifer the obvious significance of this. I concocted a story that the "H" stood for Heaven and that we, on the seventh floor were in "seventh heaven". I began to prattle on that God had a sense of humour in putting up a big "H" up there. I explained to Jennifer that we were sent by God to the seventh floor because we were close to heaven but hadn't gone that far yet. We were not meant to die at this time, I advised her, and the placement of the "H" up to the left indicated that we must look up to the left when we wanted to consult God. Jennifer inhaled everything I said and vehemently agreed. I then related to her all the details about the previous night when I thought I was going to hell and how thrilled I was to be sent here instead. She confirmed to me that I had indeed been sent by God as a saved Christian!

Jennifer was an interesting looking woman; frail, slight and obviously younger than me. Her face contained shadows under her deep set eyes and a wide mouth that revealed unhealthy teeth when she smiled. She stood about five and a half feet tall and wore several layers of hospital gowns all at once. Nevertheless, she struck me as a kind woman and we certainly reinforced each other's delusional states as we continued to chat more about the religious significance of our hospital stay. Somehow, our distorted beliefs made our stay in Seven West quite pleasant and even joyful. We decided that we were on a mission, had the healing of others to attend to and would be quite busy. I leaned on the window ledge and looked up at the "H" glowing in blue. "God's looking down on us", I told her, "but we're not going to heaven on this trip. This is a trial for us. We must act fast while we are here". These comments inspired Jennifer to get off her bed and occupy herself with the business of making her bed, adjusting the fruit in her bowl and generally moving about in the purpose of tidiness. She began talking to herself about the purpose of being a saved Christian and about the evil doers in her family that were trying to interfere with her. As she was talking, I suddenly noticed a pungent chemical smell and felt a rush of cold air. The few objects around me seemed to jump out of their settings because of vividly bright colours. Just as quickly these sensations subsided, but I told Jennifer that I might be dead and would be the last to find out. After some consoling words from her, I calmed down and sat on my bed. The feeling of heightened senses came over me periodically for the next two weeks, especially when I was watching television.

At first glance, my hospital room was stark even by minimalist standards. Fortunately I had the window seat with a bed that faced the letter "H". Jennifer's bed was beside mine and the beds were separated by an opaque curtain which could be drawn when privacy was needed. Each of the beds was dressed with a blue blanket, a clean white sheet and a single pillow. Three walls of the room were painted a dull beige, however the end wall at the foot of our beds was mauve. Both of us had a simple desk chair and we shared the singular wooden desk that was against the mauve wall. I would end up spending quite a lot of time there, studying books about bipolar disorder and reading the bible that the hospital chaplain had given me. Beside each bed stood a plain night table with drawers for magazines or personal effects. There was no art, no adornment of any kind – nothing stimulating or remotely cozy about the place, and I imagine it was intended to stay that way so as not to inspire too much comfort about remaining in the hospital long term. Neither Jennifer nor I had the luxury of fresh flowers from any visitors and therefore, the surroundings remained bare.

By all accounts, I was a good patient – this time. I was glad to be in the hospital, knew I needed to be, and was ready to follow any instructions given by the doctors and nurses. There were twenty-five patients on the unit, filling it to capacity. The ward consisted of two long, beige hallways with adjoining corridors at each end, and a floor that seemed to be continuously dirty although it was frequently swept and mopped. Each of the long halls housed the rooms of the patients – some single, some double and some wards with four patients. At the end of each hallway were the locked doors that kept patients in and others out. Between the locked doors on each side of the unit stood the nurses' station which also housed doors and windows that could be locked for private conversation or to keep patients out. Outside the station, white boards were posted indicating which nurses were assigned to each patient. Each hospital room had its own two piece bathroom, but the showers (which were filthy) were shared and we as patients had to line up to use them. Located off one of the long halls, close to the nurses' station was the cafeteria, stark and bland like the rest of the place. We as patients used it for meals, recreation or socializing. At the far end of that hall was a lounge – equipped with the only colourful items in the unit in the form of upholstered chairs and couches. A lonely plant sat drying out on one of the end tables and a second television was available to patients who didn't want to play ping pong on the table provided. Overall, the entire ward contained very little to look at save a few pictures in the hallways. It was not exactly a welcoming place and yet I felt safe and comfortable there.

Shortly after my admission to Seven West, I received a printout of expected codes of conduct and a schedule listing groups, activities and therapy as planned by the staff. Patients were required to eat all meals in the cafeteria, to take medication as prescribed and to participate in all therapeutic activities arranged for them. Women were not allowed in the men's rooms and visa versa. All socializing was to take place in the common areas. Since I am tall, I was allowed to alter my hospital garb to a degree, by wearing hospital pants with my own T-shirt and flip flops because the air was so warm. I would not be allowed to wear street clothes until I had been on the unit for seventy two hours or longer if I was considered to be unsafe. I was also not allowed off the unit to go get coffee or take a break outside for this timeframe or until I was less disoriented.

After being on the ward for about an hour, I telephoned my friend Michelle and asked her to bring some of my belongings from home, then, after she arrived, I decided to go "on rounds" and begin my delusionary mission. Wandering in the hallways for a few minutes, I stumbled upon Joseph in one of the adjoining corridors. He informed me that he was in the hospital because he had jumped onto the subway tracks and had then been apprehended by the police. I wasn't sure if he was telling me the whole story because unexpectedly he shouted, "Jesus, my saviour!" Then just as suddenly, he regained his composure.

Joseph said that he was twenty-three but his elegant appearance and articulate speech made him seem older. I informed him that I thought he would be a doctor some day. In a delusional state, I advised him of my mission and of "thought techniques" he could use to help him make decisions. I informed him (as I had done with my roommate) that to seek the word of God, he should look up to the left, for new knowledge he should look up to the right and for language he should look down to the left. I warned him that looking down to the right meant seeking guidance from the devil, and that he must avoid these glances at all costs. Of course I made all this up but was convinced that I was receiving direct messages from God! Nevertheless, Joseph took me seriously, practised the glances several times with me watching then went off to tell the others. Before he left, I warned him not to walk along the hallway on the other side of the unit because the devil was there. He thus confined his pacing to our hallway and actually his room was next to mine.

Eventually, the clock read five p.m. and an announcement came through indicating that dinner was served. Meal time provided an interesting opportunity to observe the other patients – their symptoms and behaviours. I found it fascinating! Most of the patients were extremely dishevelled, sporting dirty uncombed hair and partially unfastened attire. Many also walked with a stupor taking small slow steps, or shuffling in the direction of the tables. I wondered about their diagnoses and suspected that a good number of these patients were schizophrenic. Some talked to themselves or to people that weren't there and others were reclusive or socially inappropriate. I later found out that by being supportive and interested in the patients, I could quite easily get them to divulge their diagnoses and symptoms. This was none of my business but I found it too interesting to ignore. I had been right about the proportion who were schizophrenic but found out that there were a number of bipolar patients as well. I have always found psychiatric patients intriguing in spite of myself and in fact, I have been working with them throughout my twenty year teaching career in special education. I made an effort to remain on friendly terms with everyone, and most were as pleasant as they could be in return.

There was a great shuffling and general disorientation as everyone filed into the cafeteria. Our dinner trays included a written menu with our names typed on them at the bottom. It will come as no surprise that the food was bland, lukewarm and − well − typical hospital food if there is such a thing. (I think there is). Eventually, despite grumblings and mutterings, everyone eventually found their own tray and most of us sat down in the seats adjacent to our dinners.

One of the last patients to sit down was a woman named Shannon. Her appearance completely shocked me. She was extremely emaciated, frail and yellow in complexion. Her bleached and dirty hair stuck out like straw and looked like it hadn't been washed in weeks. She had fine hair all over her body and face and a sad, almost hopeless expression. Her primary diagnosis was anorexia nervosa and I soon found out that the status of her health was critical. Demonstrating a painfully slow shuffle and awkward gait, she was the only patient who did not actively look for her own dinner tray. She simply sat down in the first empty seat she could find. Shannon was accompanied by a staff member who was trying to implement treatment goals and get her to eat. Shannon began to vocalize her revulsion towards her food and although I expected to hear a mature woman's voice, she sounded like a squeaking, whining young child. "I don't like it", she whimpered and no attempt at reasoning with her could get her to eat. I was quite curious about Shannon but frightened by her neglect of herself. Cheerfully, I introduced myself and she squeaked a greeting to me. She then began to plead with me to have her tray taken away because, "I don't like it". Her annoying repetition of this plea was hard to take but everyone seemed to know not to bother her. I changed the subject and asked her how long she had been a patient. This time, Shannon made eye contact with me and I was quite impressed by her large chocolate brown eyes, the only soft feature on her face which was otherwise bony, angular and gaunt. She didn't have an answer for me but she did momentarily stop complaining about the food. It was my observation and interpretation that force-feeding wouldn't work for Shannon. She was as stubborn as a mule and could outlast her supervisors by a mile. However, I would attempt to use distraction in the near future to solicit appropriate behaviour from Shannon. I wondered how in the world did someone like her respond to treatment. Shannon seemed to be in a different state of consciousness, and I surmised that whoever was in charge of her treatment program would have to tap into this. At dinner, her worker didn't let her leave the table for over an hour, but Shannon's stubbornness won the battle and the worker finally gave up and left. Shannon's food, which included a full dinner and three cans of Ensure was put in the fridge.

Meanwhile, I was struggling to manage sitting beside a huge, lumbering man who was being highly inappropriate and asking me a lot of personal questions. He suddenly blurted out, "Can we be girlfriends?" Abruptly, I told him off and let him know that I would put a curse on him if he sat near me again. I was not yet based in reality either. Nevertheless, Marvin reacted fearfully toward me and quickly exited the cafeteria as soon as he'd finished eating.

After dinner, I went back to my room and found that my roommate Jennifer had brought her dinner tray back to our room in order to eat by herself. I apologized for leaving her alone, but she was not upset and said that she would just like to talk to me and not anyone else. Jennifer definitely had an agenda – to only speak to "saved Christians" and she was convinced that I was indeed "saved". Despite her psychosis (she often talked to herself or to people who weren't there), she was a kind, intelligent woman and I enjoyed our chats. At this particular time, she told me that there were evil people in her life, interfering in her business and making her miserable. These people, she said, were not "saved Christians" and Jennifer cursed them while pacing back and forth in our room. Her curses became a recurring theme in her repertoire of maladjusted behaviours.

After a few minutes of listening to Jennifer, I heard an announcement over the speaker that arts and crafts were about to begin in the cafeteria. I knew from my previous stay that this meant colouring infantile pictures with crayon and I couldn't understand why so many of the patients weren't insulted by this. At any rate, I chose not to participate but I did decide after about ten minutes to go and watch. I sincerely enjoyed observing the other patients and seeing how they interacted with each other. Surprisingly, everyone enjoyed the art activity. I couldn't get over it. After a couple of hours, I wandered back to my room, exhausted due to having spent so many nights awake. I hoped that sleep would catch up to me soon. At nine-thirty, the night nurse assigned to me arrived with my medication yet I was not yet given anything new – that would happen later, once I had seen the psychiatrist. Jennfier and I got ready for bed and by eleven o'clock we were both asleep. Fortunately, I slept uninterrupted until the next morning at seven a.m.

Shortly after awakening, my nurse came into the room and informed me that I would see my psychiatrist at nine. I asked to have a shower before breakfast and I felt much better afterwards. Breakfast presented the same puzzle as dinner had the night before, with everyone scrambling around trying to find his or her tray. Some patients were given cardboard trays and plastic cutlery for safety reasons, but I had a regular plastic tray and silverware.

Just as I was finishing my breakfast, my psychiatrist entered the cafeteria and introduced herself to me. She took me to a private room across from my own and asked me about the circumstances of my admission to Seven West. We were both clear that changes would have to be made to my medication in order to stabilize as I had experienced a full manic episode.

There are a number of drugs that can be used to treat bipolar disorder which address mood instability and psychosis. I had tried many unsuccessfully and my reluctance to take the only antipsychotic left had materialized out of my fear of weight gain. I had been lying to psychiatrists for a number of months telling them that I was allergic to the drug. However, I knew that this time I must make the sacrifice and agreed to start olanzapine (Zyprexa) the next day. Other medications such as lithium and valproate that work for other people had not worked for me and had side effects that were too problematic. This time, I felt optimistic that Zyprexa would work.

I spent my first full day in the hospital talking to Jennifer, socializing, observing others, reading and playing the odd game of cribbage. I had a selection of reading materials about bipolar disorder and poured over it in an effort to learn as much as possible.

During the course of the day, a number of patients were allowed to sign out and go off the unit for a short time or go out with family members. Since I was still so disoriented, I knew that I must stay put – this was only my second day and I was not yet on my new medication.

I left the private office and walked toward my room. Pounding and banging noises were again emanating from the room two doors from mine, and once again, three security guards were posted outside the room. The patient inside was obviously distressed and angry and likely needed to express some aggression. Suddenly, he opened the door to his room and shouted at the guards. I was floored! There stood this giant of a man, over six and a half feet tall, with a huge frame, long tangled hair, a scruffy beard and a flushed face. His hospital garb, obviously too small for him, was falling off. He began to argue with the guards, but fortunately, they succeeded in convincing him to go back into his room where his meltdown continued. Eventually, the commotion stopped, the security guards left and I didn't see this patient again until early the next morning.

The rest of the day was uneventful but I was content to be in the unit with the support I needed to fight off my demons. I made a pact with myself that I would do what I was told by the staff and that I knew they were there to help me.

The following morning, I took my first dose of Zyprexa. The plan was to have the dosage gradually increased in order to reach a target treatment level. After a few days, my hallucinations subsided although I was still somewhat delusional and remained hyper-religious for much of my stay. Fortunately, I didn't experience the dreaded side-effect of increased appetite and I was relieved. On the third evening, however, I did start experiencing some side-effects either from the new medication or from the illness itself, I'm still not sure which. After falling asleep initially, I awoke every hour or so with the sensation that a whole day had passed and that I had missed it. I also had a pounding headache for which I was fortunately given Tylenol. After a restless night, I decided to get up and make myself a cup of tea. It was four-thirty a.m. and I stayed up for the remainder of the day. Luckily, Jennifer was not disturbed by my restlessness as she was a deep and heavy sleeper.

I wandered through the hallways for a few minutes before asking the nurses if I could make tea and discovered that I was not the only patient awake. There were two others and one was fully dressed in street clothes and a leather jacket. The latter was an aloof, unfriendly and aggressive woman and I found out later that her name was April. Along with her leather jacket, she wore an old hat, faded jeans and black boots. Absorbed in her own thoughts, she was talking to herself, quite crossly, I thought. She carried a handful of notes with her and as I discovered later on, she would often write throughout the day and night and she never seemed to sleep. I found out that April refused to take medication for her illness and was hospitalized involuntarily. In addition, she had been in Seven West for months. Her personality was problematic for most patients as she could be rude or threatening. Her crossed eyes bulged out from her face as if she had hyperthyroidism but she avoided eye contact with everyone. April was very articulate but disjointed in her speech. She had her own room, perhaps due to pervasive wakefulness. She did not socialize with anyone and took her meals in her room, and the other patients remained wary of her. Instead of wandering the halls as she did, I aimed for the cafeteria. I was wide awake and alert, still manic, and I decided not to go back to bed.

When I entered the cafeteria, I got quite a surprise. There was Jack, the massive man who had been raging in his room the day before. He was dishevelled and flushed, rummaging through the kitchen drawers in search of something to eat. Sometimes, little packets of cookies could be found mixed in with teabags and pouches of instant coffee. Jack was enormous in every way – his booming voice, huge frame and large head. With matted hair and beard, he looked like a wild eyed preditor in a psychological thriller. For some reason though, I wasn't frightened. He was playing with some chess pieces so I cautiously introduced myself. He did likewise and much to my surprise, he asked me in a gentle voice if I would like to play a game of chess. Curious, I replied in the affirmative on the condition that he would do up his clothing. We set up the pieces and started our game. I soon realized that there was more to this monster than meets the eye. He was an astute chess player and articulate speaker and told me that his sister had been spying on him through a hidden camera in his home. When I probed him further about this he began to make lascivious comments about me. I didn't take them personally (Jack was schizophrenic) but scolded him anyway. Like a little boy, he apologized and referred to himself as a bad boy. I thanked him for the apology and we continued to play. With his size and volatility, I should have been terrified of Jack, but I wasn't. He was rather intriguing and seemed highly intelligent. He spoke about his secluded home, essentially a sprawling farm northeast of Toronto and indicated that he adored the peace and quiet and loved being alone. Jack had been married several years ago but the marriage fell apart when he became ill. I divulged that I was in the hospital due to a psychotic manic episode of bipolar disorder. He seemed interested and asked me questions about it. Eventually we got around to the subject of books. I am a voracious reader and can easily talk about my books. Jack stated his favourite titles and articulated, in great detail, his impressions of various authors. Obviously, he was well read and enjoyed books as much as I did. In the end, Jack won the chess game.

Seven a.m. arrived while we were talking and it started to get light. Finally, breakfast was served but I didn't see Shannon at all. Afterwards, I had a second meeting with my psychiatrist. We made up a treatment plan including therapy, medication and support services.

I continued to experience unusual side effects from either the medication or my illness. By the fourth or fifth day, the hallucinations had stopped, but the night-time awakenings with headaches continued. I also developed severe muscle aches and stiffness that required immediate physiotherapy yet the aches and pains lasted for only a day. By the fifth day, when I was allowed off the unit for short periods of time, I was still disoriented and got lost in the hospital several times. I was still waking up in the middle of the night, asking the nurses to open the cafeteria for breakfast. The nurses soon got used to guiding me back to my room with instructions to go back to sleep.

Five days passed. I still had not had one visitor nor did I feel like calling anyone. I was getting used to the effects of my medication and was spending the days reading, writing in my little black book, walking, playing games or talking with other patients. I wasn't remotely bored, anxious or rebellious. The hospital staff members were extremely good with me and I was a co-operative patient.

By the sixth day, with better mental organization, I realized that I had some responsibilities to take care of in the outside world, and I started making phone calls. One of the calls I made was to my mother. It didn't go well. The conversation became confrontational and I got upset and hung up. Her response was to repeatedly call the patient phone but I refused to answer. Some of the other patients could see that I was becoming agitated and they volunteered to answer the phone so that I wouldn't have to. Suddenly, I exploded into sobs and cried that I wanted to sue my mother for a million dollars. I called my friend Cathy to tell her. At that point, God bless her, Cathy took over and dealt with my mother and me. Meanwhile, my nurses encouraged me not to speak with my mother again during my stay at Seven West.

With the support from my new friends in the hospital, I calmed down and at that moment, I decided that I didn't want any more of the old me to surface anymore and wanted to start a new life. When I was calmer, I finally realized that I wouldn't sue my mother and after I was composed, I became so tired that I returned to my room for a nap. I had instructed the nurses not to let any more phone calls through for me. I stayed in my room for the evening and went to bed early.

The next day I was ready to begin the therapeutic component of my treatment. As patients, we had been given a schedule that included group therapy, fitness, recreation and community meetings. Most parts of the program were useful, but I found the group therapy a bit off the mark and too basic (likely due to my own training and experience in this field). Nevertheless, the program was beneficial in maintaining structure in our day, which we all needed.

After the morning fitness session, I was called to the nurses' station and informed that my mother had arranged a meeting with my psychiatrist and myself for the next day. I advised my nurse that I would not be attending the meeting. Fortunately, one of the patients passed me in the hallway and told me that I was about to be teleported to another planet! Later on, my nurse assured me that there would be no meeting without my consent. I spent the rest of the day talking to Jennifer or Shannon.

At ten a.m. the following morning, I decided to sign myself out of the unit to stroll around the hospital and get a cup of coffee. Just as I was about to exit, I was stopped by a nurse who informed me that my brother and mother had arrived and were talking to my psychiatrist. The nurse advised me that I would be expected to attend the meeting. Taken by surprise, I nevertheless consented. Upon entering the meeting room, I encountered my mother and brother seated in chairs arranged in a circle. I refused to make eye contact with my mother and she averted her gaze from me as well. My brother greeted me in a tone and manner that suggested I was a small child and I felt a bit insulted. Nevertheless, I was glad that he was there because I wasn't sure what would transpire between my mother and me.

Then my psychiatrist commenced with the meeting's agenda. Her glances towards my mother and then to me indicated that she understood the tension between us. The doctor spent a few minutes discussing my progress, symptoms and treatment plan. My mother's wish was to talk about my finances. She had a tight-lipped, stern expression on her face, not a comforting one. The discussion moved to the issue of whether I needed a power of attorney to handle my financial affairs. I had previously thought about this option following a support group meeting but certainly did not want anyone else taking control. The psychiatrist fortunately became more directive and explained that my lack of financial management was a symptom of my illness, not a wilful behaviour. I decided not to appoint a power of attorney, but to have a community support program put in place which would be overseen by my family doctor. I concluded that if I didn't take care of my finances myself, I might never know if I had the ability to do so when I got better.

About an hour later when the meeting officially ended, my brother stayed back for a few minutes to tell me that I would not be invited to Christmas dinner due to my illness and relationship with my mother. I didn't react negatively to this as I had already planned to stay in Toronto. In fact at that time, I didn't even think I'd be leaving the hospital before Christmas. My brother then left and I realized that I had made it through the meeting relatively unscathed except for the experience of ongoing tension between my mother and me. Overall, I was happy with the way my psychiatrist had conducted the session.

Afterwards, I really needed a break and asked if I could have a half day pass which meant leaving the hospital for a few hours. It was granted and I took the bus home to tidy up a bit. Fortunately, I didn't get disoriented in the community but still felt a little strange in my apartment since my last experience there had been a frightening deterioration into mania. Feeling a bit unsafe, I gingerly and slowly checked out each room and noticed that I had left things in quite a bit of disarray, and therefore spent my time organizing my space and making my apartment appear more welcoming. When I left, I realized that my first outing was a success and upon my return to the hospital, I did not, this time, get lost in the corridors!

The next day, I was granted a full day pass. Clearly, some of the other patients were getting better as well and were also granted day passes. When away from the hospital, we had to abide by a few rules which included punctuality after our outing and calling in at each location we visited. I decided to go home again. Upon entering my apartment, I still felt some discomfort and anxiety. Nevertheless, I went in, turned on the television and closed the door behind me. I had some minor auditory hallucinations but this time, I knew what they were so I didn't panic and decided to stay busy.

In keeping with the Christmas spirit (which I have too much of), I elected to dig my tree and decorations out of my storage room. I managed to put up the tree and get the lights on, then I called the hospital to let them know where I was and what time I'd be returning. I found the Christmas decorating soothing and it put me in a festive spirit. I worked at it for about four hours, but let me tell you from experience that it takes a full eighteen hours to decorate that tree and when it's finished, it is spectacular!

After decorating, I cleaned up a bit, then took my first shower at home – what a treat. To be in a nice, unshared and clean bathroom was heaven. After getting dressed, I packed up a few extra clothes to take back to the hospital with me and returned just before dinner, having had another successful outing.

After the meal and a game of cribbage with Elaine I went in search of Shannon as I had not seen her in the cafeteria. What I found was shocking. Shannon was in the observation room adjacent to the nurses' station sitting on her bed with her eye and the left side of her face blackened and bruised. I was allowed to call her out for a moment and she came shuffling towards me wearing the ratty old Winnie the Pooh socks she had worn every day so far. I asked her what happened but she didn't remember and the nurses wouldn't tell me a thing. I was growing increasingly worried about Shannon as she continued to lose weight and refused to eat. She was wasting away.

A little later on in the evening, Shannon was allowed to come to the cafeteria. I had spent most of my evenings there playing games, watching television and chatting. That evening a bunch of us were sitting around, talking and eating arrowroot cookies. I invited Shannon to join us and asked if I could make her a cup of tea. Fully expecting her to decline, I found that she accepted, and that moment was the first time I saw Shannon put anything in her mouth in a week. Not wanting to make a big deal of it and embarrass Shannon in front of the others, I hatched a plan. Occasionally, I would put a few arrowroots in front of her then pretend not to notice her actions. It worked. Shannon opened the first package and began to eat. She had become so engrossed in our conversation that she totally forgot herself. She started to become talkative and animated and continued to eat the cookies. The other patients and I were all very happy to witness this. Shannon and I stayed in the cafeteria until eleven thirty when the lights were turned out. It had been a successful day on all fronts, and exhausted, I went back to my room, took my medication and fell into bed. I slept normally (which is not normal for me).

The next day my psychiatrist instructed me to take an overnight pass at my apartment. I wasn't sure that I was ready for this as I still had some anxieties about hallucinating when there alone. But I agreed to give it a try. When I arrived there, I gave a few friends a call to update them on my condition. Most of them did not know that I had been admitted to a psychiatric ward or that I had experienced a psychotic episode. It felt good to touch base with people from the outside world, however, I spent the rest of the day and evening by myself, strangely, completing the decoration of my Christmas tree and putting up various other seasonal ornaments. I can't accurately recall what that night was like for me but it must have been reasonably successful, as I returned to the hospital promptly the next day in a positive mood. My friend Jack, who also got better in the past few days was completely transformed in appearance when I arrived back to the unit. His outing had been a success as well and he was dressed completely in neat street clothes and sported a short haircut and fresh shave. I almost didn't recognize him.

The next day was the Tuesday of my second week in the hospital. I had almost forgotten what the days of the week were and tended to identify them by number based on my date of admission. It was day nine. On medication that worked, I was stable enough to be considered for release. In the morning, my psychiatrist advised me that I would stay in the hospital for two more days and that I must participate in all groups and programs for the remainder of the time. Jennifer, my roommate had been released while I was on my overnight, so I had a room to myself for the remainder of the time.

I felt this time that I had achieved an improved state of wellness while in Seven West. I had read a great deal, and had written a lot in my strange little black notebook as well. When I reread it, I was quite shocked to witness how disjointed my thoughts and speech had been at the crux of my illness. I have kept these notes and I do reread them occasionally to remind myself how far I have come since that time.

Finally, my day of departure arrived. In the morning, I packed up my belongings, including many books and initiated saying my goodbyes to everyone. For almost two weeks these patients (twenty-five in all) had been my family and friends and my departure was emotional. When I went to say farewell to Shannon, I was glad that I had been privileged to witness her begin her recovery from anorexia. Soon, she would be released as well and would move into a women's group home.

I gave her a hug and a Christmas present that I had made, and for a moment, I thought she would never let go. We exchanged phone numbers, but I did not know where Shannon would be living, and as it turned out, I would never hear from her again.

Having wished my friends well, I signed out, retrieved my release papers from the nurses' station and closed the doors of Seven West behind me. I was going home and looking forward to a new and improved life.

CHAPTER 3
A BIT OF HISTORY

By all accounts, I had a normal childhood. I was born and raised in Kitchener, Ontario and was privileged to have a wide variety of experiences throughout my youth. I was taken places, had many lessons (perhaps too many) and did well in school. I had a brother, one year younger and lived in a large, beautiful home surrounded by a huge yard and backing onto a park. My father was an interesting character, a respected lawyer and intellectual and an avid reader of science and philosophy. He loved young children, and as a result, my brother and I would wait with much anticipation towards his return home at the end of each working day. My mother, who had studied fine art was highly creative and initiated endless unique activities for the neighbourhood children and us. She struggled with a number of health conditions however and as a result, we had nannies for five years to help with the childrearing.

I was an inquisitive but shy child, yet as early as age three, I can recall being a vessel for information and my parents encouraged this by providing me with as many learning opportunities as possible. By the age of six, I displayed symptoms of Tourette's Syndrome although I wasn't diagnosed or treated until age thirty. As a youngster, I was teased because of my tics but I learned how to cope with the help of good friends and teachers. In elementary school, I skipped a grade along with a group of friends and was glad of this because many of my friends were a year older than me and the work was appropriately challenging in the higher grade.

My tenth year marked the beginning of the end for my family. My parents began to argue almost daily at increasingly escalated levels of verbal aggression. My mother would often take the role of the silent instigator and my father would over-react as the victim, and he often declared that my mother was driving him crazy. In his defence, he would call her names, but her rebuttal was stone cold silence. There was so much hatred in the air you could cut it with a knife. Heated conflicts would erupt at the slightest provocation and neither parent was really interested in or able to resolve difficulties. In these situations, my brother would either bolt from the house or up to his loft, but, my skyrocketing anxiety drove me to play the mediator and attempt to make peace. I was afraid to leave my parents alone for fear that someone would get physically hurt, but because of my interference, I often became the target during these altercations. Feelings of anger, fear, sadness and despair tormented me during family fights and I felt very unsafe, especially at night when the verbal violence was most abusive.

By the end of my elementary school years, I was desperately unhappy in my family life but the already precarious situation just continued to get worse. My mother's anger spilled over into her relationship with me and my father did not stand up for himself or protect me. As a result of the stress, I would get awful stomach aches walking home from school in anticipation of what might happen when my father got home from work. I hated being a child of feuding parents. Their anger and hatred was like a thick black cloak over my head suffocating me to the point where I couldn't breathe.

As I approached adolescence, I became an angry, opinionated and verbal youngster when at home and my stress level reached a fevered pitch. My moods were unstable and I couldn't sleep. My mother would often punish me by making me complete hours of chores to ridiculously exacting standards, and by sending my friends away when they came to call. Many of my friends were actually afraid of her. I know I certainly was. At school however, I had support, especially from my friend Cathy who had an unusual family situation of her own. Deep down however, I was enraged, vengeful and rebellious and I wanted to leave home. By the time I was thirteen, I had a plan to get out if necessary but, it wasn't very realistic. Where would I stay? What would I eat? Where would my money come from? Certainly my part-time job at the doughnut shop would not suffice.

To add insult to injury, my father began drinking excessively to deal with the stressors in his life which were familial and professional. He often drank with a neighbourhood friend who was also an alcoholic and eventually died of his affliction. My father's drunken behaviour and mood swings became unpredictable, ranging from staggering and slurred speech to full blown rages and destructive actions like dumping all of our house plants onto newly cleaned carpets or threatening my mother's safety. His intoxicated behaviour was highly frightening, and when I saw him stumble into the house after a binge, I knew I would have to brace myself for what could happen.

My father was an unusual character, probably bipolar, but he refused to seek help for his drinking problem or his unpredictable mood swings. He could work at a feverish pitch at the office, then at home would brood about his personal problems. I witnessed him having several breakdowns when I was a teenager and I was petrified, mostly about what I thought he would do to himself or my mother. He never attacked me but I stayed out of the way when he was drunk barricading myself inside my room. As far as I know, my dad never completely gave up the alcohol, even years later when he had divorced my mother and married someone else.

My adolescence was characterized by wide discrepancies in my own mood. At home, I was rebellious and defiant until about age sixteen when I developed better coping strategies and started talking to others about my problems. My teachers and friends fortunately saw a more positive side of me. I continued to be a good student, self motivated and driven by my own desire to achieve. I had long ago given up trying to please my family. Since I did not receive praise or encouragement from either parent, I learned to work hard in order to make sure that I built strong skills which would enable me to function without family support in the near future. There were many times when I nearly shut down emotionally at home, but school became my safety zone. Fortunately, I had chosen a positive peer group to socialize with although only a few knew what I was experiencing with my family.

During my last years at high school, both my parents had affairs and their marriage irretrievably broke down. By this time, I was numb emotionally and almost looked forward to the breakup. I have often felt that my personal and emotional development was stunted by my experiences with my family, and that I failed to reach some important milestones. What I didn't know was that my dad likely suffered from undiagnosed bipolar disorder and that symptoms were beginning to emerge in me as well. As a result, I have historically made poor choices in developing relationships with men or else have remained single. (Judgment is often highly impaired in bipolar individuals).

By the time my parents separated, I was nineteen, in university and frankly, relieved about the breakup. As far as my own bipolar symptoms were concerned, the insomnia continued to worsen until the middle of my freshman year at university when it spiralled out of control. The resulting exhaustion and anxiety drove me to make a career changing decision to switch from hard science to psychology. In retrospect, this was a wise decision for a number of reasons. The concepts I learned as a psychology major enabled me to develop further coping skills which I may not have had access to had I remained in biology. Secondly, psychology was really where my interest lay and I was good at working with people and detecting the foundations of their numerous interpersonal problems.

Once my parents separated, I thought they might perhaps have time to take an interest in getting to know me but I was mistaken and disappointed. Both of them had become self centered, nurturing their affairs instead of their children, and they could not offer the kind of support necessary to direct a youngster on the best road to adulthood. As a result, my relationship with my parents became superficial. Within a few years, my father remarried a much younger woman and had a son by her. My mother continued her long affair with a married man.

Four years later, I graduated with an honours degree in Applied Science (psychology), then worked for one year at a closed custody group home as a counsellor for delinquent adolescent girls. Although I was not as disturbed as my clients were, I could easily relate to their anger, manipulation and poor decision making. They were tough street kids and accordingly, I had to toughen up as well, but the girls taught me a lot and I formed strong treatment bonds with them, even with the violent ones. After a year of that experience, I moved to Toronto to study education and become a special education teacher.

At twenty-four I got married, which was a huge mistake for me because of my lack of positive experiences with men. I didn't love my husband but thought my indifference would pass. It didn't. Within this relationship, I either felt agitated or depressed and numb. As a result of poor insight, my shaky new marriage quickly fell into boring routine and I reacted by building up my life outside the home. In addition, I didn't have the emotional maturity to face the problems my marital relationship presented. My time was spent taking courses, shopping, crafting Christmas decorations, engaging in sports, visiting friends and eventually having an affair myself, with a younger man – a poor judgment call admittedly, but my mood skyrocketed as a result. I felt alive again, had a new zest for living and fell in love with this young man. I suppose I always knew that this relationship wouldn't last but for the time being, I felt loved and respected. Having the affair seemed easy. I got used to lying to my husband and he took little notice of me anyway. Therefore, I became a Jeckyl and Hyde personality. Eventually however, I realized that my new boyfriend had a great many personal problems for which he didn't have the intelligence or conviction to solve – problems like alcohol and drug abuse, lack of education, chronic unemployment and family issues.

After a year of my two-faced behaviour, I started having panic attacks as reality set in, and worried that I would have to give up both relationships and live alone. The attacks progressively intensified and increased in frequency. No longer could I think clearly and I was weaving a web of deception with both men and also with myself. I was at an impasse and couldn't seem to make any decisions at all, being unable to control my moods from one moment to the next.

One day (subconsciously perhaps) I made a fatal mistake. My husband came home early from a long distance business trip, sensing something was wrong, only to find my boyfriend in our apartment. In a rage, my husband broke the door down and physically attacked us both. The neighbours next door heard me screaming and called the police. My boyfriend managed to get away and I ran to the neighbours' apartment and waited for the police to arrive. I was in absolute shock and disbelief over what had just transpired. My husband had thrown me against a wall and torn my clothing. I felt petrified and feared for my life.

When the police arrived, they placed a restraining order on him and ordered him to leave town to stay with his parents for the next few nights in Kitchener. Then they attempted to talk to me but I remained traumatized and dumbfounded. What had I done? Why didn't I realize that I was in trouble before all this happened? That night I was alone, frightened and panicked because my behaviour had become the cause of this violent incident. I slept only fitfully and called in sick at work the next morning. I was teaching at a private school at the time. Paralyzed by fear and anxiety, I could not think or function at all so I called my family in Kitchener to ask for their help. My father and brother came to pick me up in Toronto and delivered me to my mother's home. Suffering crippling panic by this point, I was out of control and desperately needed help.

A few days after I arrived in Kitchener myself, it somehow was arranged that my husband and I would visit his church pastor for counselling – together! I was clearly very sick and confused and very depressed. I recall my husband announcing in this session that he would only use violence as a last resort in a relationship – and he had. His pastor was taken aback that he even considered violence as an option and counselled him about this. When it was my turn to speak, the pastor told me that in order to heal, I would have to give up my affair and call my boyfriend from his church to tell him that I was saying goodbye. I experienced the most intense, gut wrenching emotional pain I'd ever felt while contemplating this loss.

Soon, a deep depression set in and I started having panic attacks only minutes apart. Disoriented and with much difficulty, I drove back to my mother's home and my husband drove to the home of his parents. I had no idea what I was going to do, where I would live and how to cope with this devastating mess. My heart and my head had failed me at the same time. For a week, I stayed on with my mom while my husband drove back to Toronto to go back to work. My mom helped make arrangements for me to stay temporarily with a friend of hers in Toronto so that I could return to work as well. However, the debilitating symptoms of my illness made me feel literally like I was going to die and I fell into a growing sense of unreality and doom. I was suffering gripping panic attacks a few times per hour at this point. The crushing chest pain, shortness of breath, stomach aches, sweating and disorganized thinking were insurmountable symptoms.

Recognizing my need for help, I called my family doctor and got a referral to see a local psychiatrist. In our first meeting, she could see that I was so out of control that she immediately prescribed several medications at once for anxiety and depression. The symptoms did not abate at all. I felt that I had no future, that I might as well be dead. I was barely able to teach the children who were my charges and I had no home.

One night while I was staying at my mother's friend's house in Toronto, my husband turned up at her door when I was there alone. He was livid and began screaming and raging at me, so loudly that one of the neighbours called the police. I was terrified, as my husband aggressively grabbed my left hand and attempted to pull off my wedding ring. When I got away from him he let forth hideous howls, but the police arrived within a couple of minutes and ordered him to leave. At that point, I felt that my life might be in danger and I shook violently. The next day, my mother's friend (no doubt disturbed by the events of the previous evening) informed me that I would have to move out since she felt that I was being stalked by my husband and didn't want to be in any danger herself. In actual fact, he had been stalking me in the community and had left lengthy, manipulative letters in my car. I wondered how he had found me wherever I happened to be in the city – perhaps he had hired a private investigator to follow me. I never found out. Highly disturbed about the recent events, I contacted my lawyer who advised me to send the letters directly to him – unopened.

Out of control, I continued to see my psychiatrist but failed to respond to the medication she prescribed. I was quickly losing hope that I would live through the next few days and weeks. I was terrified that my husband could be dangerous if provoked. Nevertheless, I had to move back in with him and the whole experience was completely absurd. I certainly wasn't getting any better. Then after about three months, I started to feel a bit more mentally organized and was clear-headed enough to make the decision to leave my husband for good. Finally, the medication started working for me. I began to relax and feel that I might possibly have a future after all. I would make it on my own no matter what! This change in me happened on a sunny November morning while I was driving to work. Everything happened within a moment. I knew what I had to do. The panic attacks suddenly stopped and I knew right then that I must never look back. I made a plan to see my psychiatrist with my husband present so that I could tell him my decision. Because of his previous violent behaviour, I didn't feel safe enough to tell him in an unsupervised setting.

That same evening after work, I drove to my psychiatrist's office alone. I could feel the adrenalin coursing through my veins. By the time I got to the office, my husband was already there. Without looking at him, I sat down, with butterflies in my stomach but also with a firm plan to terminate the relationship. When the session began, I calmly and resolutely stated that I would be leaving my husband permanently. Immediately upon hearing this, he flew into a rage, threatened both the therapist and myself, and stormed out of the office. My heart and head raced as I quickly formulated a plan with the therapist. My whole body was shaking. From the psychiatrist's office, I called my aunt as well as the police and informed them that I would need support in getting some of my belongings out of the apartment. I did not feel safe enough to attempt this on my own. I didn't know if my husband would be home, but if so, I suspected that he might be dangerous. Leaving the doctor's office, I drove home and met my aunt and two police officers in the outdoor parking lot of my building. My heart was still racing. We went upstairs to the apartment and I saw that the lock had already been changed. The apartment also looked dark – there was no light shining through the space at the bottom of the door. I knocked – no answer. After a few attempts, the police took over. They assumed that because of the new lock, my husband would indeed be inside. The officers demanded that my husband open the door but he did not. Then came the threat that they would break down the door if he did not comply. Slowly, the door creaked open. The apartment was enveloped in darkness. My husband had a bottle of rye in his hand and was clearly drunk and seething with anger. Both officers escorted him to a chair and instructed him to sit down. He looked awful. They gave my aunt and me fifteen minutes to get what I needed for a couple of weeks of living elsewhere. The officers then placed another restraining order on my husband and advised him not to attempt to contact or follow me. My aunt and I hurried to the bedroom to gather up some articles of clothing and a few possessions. The plan was that I would stay at her place in Toronto for the next few days while I looked for suitable accommodation.

Within fifteen minutes, the two of us left accompanied by the police officers and that was it. It was over. When we arrived back at my aunt's apartment, I felt relieved to be safe but also a bit bizarre and disoriented and was likely in some sort of shock again. That night, I couldn't sleep and had a momentary but powerful relapse into anxiety and panic. At about two in the morning, I took extra medication to get me back on track but I accidently overdosed and became sick to my stomach. Gradually, as the night progressed, the symptoms subsided, I settled down and was able to catch a couple of hours of sleep in the early morning hours.

Feeling a little better after sleeping a bit, I got up, still certain of my decision and went to work. I felt a little unsure of myself but finally, by noon, I was able to eat my lunch for the first time in a long while and was better able to teach without falling apart. While at work that day, I had to immediately start planning and thinking about finding a new place to live. After leaving my aunt's apartment a few days later, having slept on her couch, I still had nowhere to live so I stayed with my mother in Kitchener for a couple of weeks and commuted three hours each way to my teaching placement in Queensville. It was exhausting.

Eventually, I found a peculiar little apartment in downtown Newmarket, a location closer to my school. Since I had just started this teaching position and was still recovering, I did not want to live too great a distance from work. The apartment was far from luxurious and was in a neighbourhood (I found out later) surrounded by halfway houses, group homes and low income housing. The building was old – it had been a converted ice house with warped floors and live wires under the sink – a problem for which I had to call the fire department. Most of the tenants in this building were on welfare and the woman who lived across the hall from me was a drunk. Once I realized the nature of the situation I had got myself in to, I broke down into tears and felt lost. Happily, my mother came to Newmarket to help me paint and clean up for a few days and the place slowly transformed into a home for me, which wasn't great but it was manageable.

Gradually, I continued to get better and better following the termination of my marriage but still remained very puzzled about what had been wrong with me – the panic attacks, disorientation, inability to eat, indecisiveness and depression. I had made some poor decisions, but I was also curious about what had happened to my brain and mind and since I was still on medication, I wondered if I had some kind of psychiatric diagnosis. I began to research the matter fervently, and thus began my journey into reading, a new habit which, as it turns out, would stay with me for life.

Because of my research and one more visit to my psychiatrist I discovered that my diagnosis was called agitated depression. I didn't know at the time that I was in fact bipolar. I devoured every book and article I could find on depression and anxiety and poured over the information until I felt properly educated. Gradually, over the next few months under the supervision of my doctor, I reduced and then stopped taking medication, however, a few weeks later, I started to experience anxiety again. Wondering what had transpired, I went back on antidepressant medication again and have never discontinued it since.

Teaching gradually started to become more manageable and even enjoyable so I began the steps to rebuilding my life. First of all, I found my living situation in Newmarket to be too depressing, So I moved back to Toronto into a lovely, spacious, bright apartment. I got back together with my boyfriend for a time, but the relationship eventually became very unstable, and as I got better, I outgrew it. So I moved on.

At first, I found it difficult to be single and sometimes felt lonely since I had never lived on my own, but over time, I got used to it. I focussed on being physically and mentally engaged by joining a gym and by throwing myself into my work. I also pursued a life-long dream of slalom waterskiing, and fortunately became skilled at it.

So why was I still having ups and downs? It didn't make sense. I had made life-altering decisions and certainly felt more clear headed, but even after some time had passed, I would occasionally have relapses and couldn't figure out the cause of them. My teaching career helped me a great deal by giving me something meaningful to focus on, and I read a lot about behaviour and mental illness. Many of my children had serious mental health problems of their own, but because of my experience with depression and an in-depth study of mental health issues, I felt better able to empathize with them and teach them coping strategies. As a matter of fact, I remained a special education teacher throughout my career and loved the challenge of helping the children develop their strengths and deal with their disabilities as well as discovering their unique gifts.

When I was thirty-one and diagnosed with Tourette's Syndrome, my parents began to wake up to my needs and we started to untangle the mess that characterized my family. Unfortunately, my father and I had little time to get to know each other. After fighting a long battle with cancer, he died shortly after the turn of the century. My dad had suffered a great deal in his life and had difficulty looking after his health. His addiction to cigarette smoking perpetuated his illness and eventual death. He is sadly missed.

One thing that always baffled me growing up was that neither of my parents ever expressed the wishes that I should be happy in life. I didn't consciously even realize that I needed to start endeavouring to be happy until I started teaching. I extended my research by beginning to read self-help books about happiness, and searched for it in relationships with others and worked towards it in my studies. But my emotions were highly chaotic and happiness remained elusive in some respects. I knew how to be a good friend and how to choose good friends but had no clue about how to have a healthy relationship with the opposite sex. I ended up making some major decisions in life which led to devastating results because of what I failed to learn about relationships as a youngster. I ended up dating just about anyone who would go out with me and had my life threatened several times because I didn't know how to connect with someone who would be good for me.

As time passed, I continued to wonder about my symptoms. In my personal life, I decided to remain single and after my relationship with my post-marital boyfriend fizzled out, I eventually became used to the single life and content with being on my own. I haven't really done anything yet about changing my social situation. Instead I have become a voracious reader and have had good friends and family members to see at other times.

Occasionally, however, I would find myself getting overexcited about things and would get wild ideas racing through my head and would stay awake for days at a time. I also loved shopping and therefore never managed to save any money, spending it as fast as I made it. Living from paycheque to paycheque, I got heavily into debt by overusing my credit card. I was never able to pay off the minimum balance because when any money came in, I would spend it. I didn't really know why I behaved like this. In the back of my mind I knew it was wrong but I couldn't seem to stop. Later I would learn how this atrocious financial behaviour would become a symptom of my diagnosis of bipolar disorder. For the time being however, I was dealing with Tourette's Syndrome and pervasive anxiety.

During my mid thirties and early forties, there were days when I couldn't get out of bed or take care of myself and periodically I felt unloved, worthless, useless and depressed. At these times I would write in a personal journal that I would take to my appointments with the Tourette's psychiatrist. I arranged more meetings with him when I was depressed and sleepless than I did at any other time. At times I would feel that my antidepressant medication wasn't working. I thought I was experiencing residual symptoms of Tourette's Syndrome and didn't realize at the time that I was heading towards serious mental illness.

In total, I saw that psychiatrist for thirteen years, tried to go off medication two more times unsuccessfully, then, towards the end of my treatment sessions with him, he communicated that I might have some symptoms of bipolar disorder. I did not understand the ramifications of this and I didn't know much about it – except that it used to be called manic depression. The doctor told me that I was talking excessively, too quickly and in a pressured way. I was rather taken aback and said that I wanted a second opinion.

I was referred to a neurologist, who upon seeing me, agreed with my psychiatrist and after a long interview, diagnosed me with bipolar II disorder, which is a milder form of the illness. I didn't agree with the neurologist since I thought I was normal, except for periodic mild depressions. I didn't realize that others saw my behaviour as erratic, aberrant and bizarre. Therefore, I poured over the research again. Meanwhile, I was placed on lithium, a common mood stabilizer and thus read as much as I could about the medication and the disorder. I knew some other people who were on lithium, yet a short time after starting the drug, I began to have trouble with side effects and felt like I had lost my personality. I felt defiant and didn't want to co-operate with the doctors. (I will go into more depth on the effects of the medication in the chapters ahead on diagnosis and treatment.) I also felt angry that I was moving from one mental illness to another and the boundaries between Tourette's Syndrome and bipolar disorder were fuzzy to me. Yet, with Tourette's in remission I shifted my focus completely towards bipolar disorder: the diagnosis, treatment and medication. I tried one more medication called valproate but demonstrated little improvement on it and my hair started to fall out. Therefore, it was discontinued.

For the next few months, I muddled through without the supervision of any psychiatrists. It was during this time that I started to have problems with memory loss and disorientation as well as recurring changes in temperament. I demonstrated outbursts of unpredictable behaviour which angered and embarrassed others. Agitated, I decided to move from my current home in Richmond Hill back to the same address I had lived at in Toronto fifteen years earlier. At the same time, I gave up my car because of the expense and also because of increasing disorientation and fatigue. Lapses of memory increased in frequency and to this date I cannot recall many events that transpired from the winter of 2005 to the following winter. By March of 2006 I knew that I was in dreadful shape, oscillating between depression and agitation. Others reported that I was making up fantastical stories about events in my life and that I was out of control. For example, after an assessment at a sleep clinic, I told friends and family that I had acquired

Parkinson's disease. This was completely untrue but somehow I even believed it myself. Another bizarre story involved a shopping trip to a local mall where I spent my entire paycheque on stuff I didn't need. As the adrenalin surged, I squandered thousands of dollars on clothing and books leaving nothing left to pay my bills or rent. Waiting at the bus stop, loaded down with shopping bags, I concocted a story in my head that I had been assaulted in the parking lot and robbed of over three thousand dollars. I whipped up some tears and when I got on the bus, I told the driver my story. He immediately stopped the bus and called his supervisor and the police. When the police arrived, I recounted my tale, even concocting a description of my imagined assailant. My story must have sounded authentic because the police wrote a full report, then drove me home, after one of the patrons on the bus said he felt sorry for me and actually gave me four hundred dollars. If I had been found out, I could have been charged with public mischief. Strangely, when I fabricated stories like this, I believed them as if they were factual.

One day in early May, I woke up feeling horrendous. I was anxious, agitated, disoriented and upset, and felt that I had lost control of my mind. Under the advice of my friend Cathy, who I telephoned at her place of work, I ran across the street to my doctor's office. My hysteria alarmed him and he instructed me to get to the emergency department of the nearest hospital right away. The next thing I can remember is that I was inside the emergency ward in a stark isolation room arguing and shouting at the on-call psychiatrist who was trying to assess me. Cathy was present at the hospital as well. Part of my psychiatric assessment consisted of a verbal report which Cathy made to the doctor. I in turn became highly paranoid because I couldn't hear what she and the psychiatrist were talking about and I assumed that the conversation was damning. Nevertheless, after being given a sedative, I became less aggressive and calmed down.

Upon realizing that I was about to be admitted to the locked psychiatric facility in the hospital, I felt completely defeated. Even though I had experienced so many difficult times in the past few years, I would do anything to avoid hospitalization and that's what I was arguing about. However, as I gradually became calmer, I eventually accepted the fact that I was staying and within the hour was taken up to Seven West, the locked psychiatric unit.

The hospital room I was escorted to was furnished only with a single bed and had annoying fluorescent lighting and white walls with no window. This was one of two crisis observation rooms and I was informed that I would be moving into a regular room the next day. I was told to put on a hospital gown and then all of my possessions were taken away from me. All through the night, I was under observation by the nurses and didn't get a wink of sleep.

Despite my wakefulness, I stayed in bed for the most part except for a few trips to the bathroom. At those times, I was supervised by a nurse and wasn't allowed to close the door. I may have actually dozed off a bit towards morning but was awakened by a doctor at six a.m. who came in to interview me. He explained that I would see a psychiatrist later that morning and would move into a room with one roommate.

At eight a.m., all patients reported to the cafeteria for breakfast. This was the first time I saw any of the other patients and most were clad in hospital gowns. I felt more normal that morning but essentially kept to myself. I noted that many patients were highly dishevelled and unclean and many walked with a stupor or shuffle, and I suspected that they had diagnoses which were much more severe than mine. I didn't know what my own diagnosis was at that time or that it was serious. After breakfast, I returned to my room and slept a bit.

Several hours later, my assigned psychiatrist met with me and conducted a lengthy psychiatric interview. We discussed my previous diagnosis of bipolar II disorder, my family's psychiatric history and the treatments I'd tried that hadn't worked. I was lucid and coherent during our talk and he wasn't really sure what I had. Nevertheless, he prescribed a new medication called risperidone which is often used as a mood stabilizer or as a treatment for Tourette's Syndrome. Within a few days, the only change I noticed was that I felt quite bloated and was not sure whether the medication was doing anything for me. My behaviour was still somewhat agitated and very disorganized. Just prior to this hospital admission, I had become an "Avon lady" and had brought all of my paperwork to the hospital with me. I kept pouring over orders that I had, shuffling papers, adding up figures and checking them over. I worked on this for hours and yet got nowhere. Much to the nurses' displeasure, I tried to sell Avon products to all of the patients until I was reprimanded by the doctor for being a nuisance.

Throughout the first week of my hospital stay, my doctors continually tried to figure out my diagnosis but were stumped. In clinical interviews, I was composed and articulate yet I was certainly still demonstrating unusual behaviour on the unit and was generally unsettled. However, it was unclear to them whether or not I was actually bipolar. In therapeutic discussion groups, I was always eager to be the patient "leader" and to share the volumes of knowledge I had about psychiatric disorders. However, I was more obnoxious than helpful. I would also direct patients to take showers or fix their hair until I was told by the nurses that this was highly offensive and inappropriate. Sometimes, I even yelled at unresponsive patients. To visitors, I appeared jubilant and hyperactive, but eventually, having spread my belongings out all over the room, my roommate found me so annoying that she asked to be placed in a different room.

After the first week of my hospital stay had passed, my mother and aunt came to visit me and I sent them to my apartment to fetch more clothing for me. I should let the reader know that I was dressing in a bizarre fashion at the time. I wore outfits entirely of one colour (for example; orange skirt, orange top, orange shoes, orange costume jewellry and even orange makeup). I begged my family to bring me five of these complete outfits and instead of talking some sense into me, they obliged. Other patients told me that I looked bizarre but I ignored them, agitated by their comments. For the remainder of my hospital stay,

I wore these loud, ridiculous outfits of purple, pink, orange, green and turquoise. Eventually, I called these my "sick clothes". I got rid of them once I was better.

After my first week as an inpatient, I didn't realize it, but I was not getting well. Instead, I was overbearing, demanding, overly gregarious and rude. I don't remember much about the passing of time during the last few days of this hospital stay. Even after my dosage of risperidone was increased, I continued to portray essentially the same high-strung temperament. After a week, I wanted out. I had attended all the required group and individual therapy sessions and felt that I couldn't gain anything more just by staying longer. I had been given permission to leave the psychiatric unit at times and was chomping at the bit to go home and start a new furniture business! I had to go "now" or I would lose my window of opportunity. (Of course, the furniture business was a hefty delusion).

As soon as I found out that I was a voluntary patient, I informed my psychiatrist that I would be leaving the next day and asked for my discharge papers to be ready. The doctor did not try to stop me, but was not in agreement that I should be discharged, and therefore, did not sign the release papers. I was not having any of this and became impatient and argumentative with staff. I signed myself out the next morning, highly agitated that the paperwork wasn't ready on time. I told the nurses that I had a business deal I needed to close by noon that day and if I didn't make it to my business location on time, I would lose five thousand dollars.

This was all nonsense of course. I was completely delusional to think of myself as such an important business person. Nevertheless, I left in a huff without consent. Because I was so distressed and self absorbed, I do not remember much about what was going on around me after my discharge. After a couple of days, I started to experience disturbing symptoms – slurred speech, blurred vision and a poor sense of balance. Worried, I called my hospital psychiatrist and left a message about the state I was in. Within the hour, a police officer was at my door with orders to escort me back to the hospital. I was placed in the crisis room of the emergency department and was supervised by two security guards. The doctor on call insisted that I drink large quantities of water, possibly to dilute my medication. When a different psychiatrist finally met me several hours later, he took me off the risperidone and prescribed yet another medication called quetiapine (Seroquel). Later that afternoon, I was discharged and given the name of a psychiatrist I would see to continue treatment as an out-patient. I still regularly see that psychiatrist to this day.

For three weeks following my discharge, I participated in an out-patient day treatment program at the hospital. Poor judgment continued to be one of my problems, but I felt that once again, I should be leading the discussions – that I was better informed than the staff. Needless to say, I was reprimanded several times for attempting to dominate the group. Following this three week session, I was advised to participate in yet another day treatment program at a different hospital. After the first day, I quit because

I thought it was a step down in quality from the first program and after all, I wasn't sick, or so I thought.

Summer finally came. I spent much of my time by my swimming pool, managed to get a bit of exercise and somehow muddled through the season (I have always felt better in summer). Frankly, I cannot recall many events of those few months, except that somehow, I made a new friend, Jasmine, who stuck with me even though I was really unwell.

Then fall arrived. I found myself depressed and weepy on some days. Spending money in order to cheer myself up, I didn't think logically about where the money was coming from or how I would pay my rent or my bills. I just spent. People around me found my behaviour bizarre and unpredictable. I started to feel very strange and uneasy. I was also severely in debt. My indiscriminate spending continued, and I became defensive and confrontational with people. I hardly slept and became completely disoriented. During the few hours of sleep that I did get, I suffered from night terrors and nightmares. In the daytime, I started getting lost in the community, forgetting when to get off buses and losing track of where I was going. I would arrive at various locations and not know how I got there. I started hearing noises and voices in my apartment and kept calling the police because I thought I heard someone trying to break in. I was clearly on my way to rock bottom, emotionally and behaviourally, and was about to embark on a most unpleasant journey – the one that took me to hell and back.

PART TWO

CHAPTER 4
DIAGNOSIS

"Would somebody please tell me what's wrong with me? Everyone is against me. My friends won't talk to me and my family members keep telling me what to do".

Bipolar disorder is considered to be an affective illness, that is, one of the disorders of mood or feeling. People with this illness experience depressions much deeper and mood elevations of mania much higher than do normal people. At some point in their lives, many individuals without bipolar disorder experience moderate depression or jubilation. They may also experience periods of great energy and creativity which motivate them to achieve great things. This emotional state may be similar to hypomania, a lower level of mania which often occurs prior to the full blown mania experienced by so many bipolar patients. In moderation, feelings of mild depression or elation may actually be adaptive and helpful. However, severe mania and/or severe depression can result in catastrophic outcomes including suicide if not treated and managed effectively.

Bipolar disorder involves extreme mood swings, from devastating depressions to acute mania. Interestingly, I also experience the illness as a fluctuation in energy levels, from manic highs punctuated by sleepless nights, bursts of creativity and strange behaviour, to depressive lows where I can barely function at all.

Bipolar disorder comes in several forms such as bipolar I disorder, bipolar II disorder, mixed states and cyclothymia. As my illness progressed, it actually changed forms, from bipolar II disorder which includes depression and hypomania, to bipolar I disorder consisting of depression and full-blown mania.

This illness used to be called manic depression and some people may be more familiar with this term. However, no diagnostic label is perfect. Some people are offended by labels, and yet a diagnosis of bipolar disorder opens up lines of communication among doctors, between doctors and patients and between researchers. Correct diagnosis leads to appropriate treatment and prognosis.

An American compendium called the Diagnostic and Statistical Manual of Mental Disorders, fourth edition (or DSM IV) outlines the criteria and conditions for the various forms of the illness. The DSM IV breaks down the components of bipolar disorder into specific symptoms and identifies the difference between bipolar I disorder and bipolar II disorder. One thing the manual does not do is explain exactly how family history affects diagnosis or how long-term patterns of the illness run their course. Again, diagnosis tends to be more accurate following hypomania and mania than it is following depression.

The DSM IV is published by the American Psychiatric Association and is intended to be used as a diagnostic tool for trained specialists with a great deal of experience in interpreting the language of the manual. In 1952, the DSM I was first published. By 1980, the third edition contained the first of the diagnostic criteria for psychiatric disorders that define each condition and separate them from each other.

Conducting an accurate diagnosis of bipolar disorder requires both a long term history of the patient as well as a look at the patient's current symptoms. Bipolar disorder is a different illness from unipolar depression and necessitates different treatment. In addition, physicians or psychiatrists need to meet with the patient frequently and help him or her identify as many symptoms as possible. Since there does seem to be some correlation between the patient's symptoms and those of family members, detailed interviews and psychiatric histories should be taken from them. Individuals who seek help for unipolar depression should also be assessed for bipolar disorder since the two separate illnesses invite different treatment.

Mania and Bipolar I Disorder

Mania exists in two forms – hypomania and mania. In each form the person experiences a mood of elation which is out of proportion to reality. Thoughts often race from one to the other and speech is often forced or rapid. Motor activity might also increase in the form of gestures, grimacing and overall movement. In hypomania, the least severe type, the person appears to be in an elated mood but doesn't seem to be out of control. Nevertheless, the mood becomes unstable and can escalate to a high degree of agitation. In mania, the mood disturbance is more pronounced and easily discerned by others but not by the patient. Behaviour becomes more inappropriate and may include reckless spending, sexual promiscuity, rude comments, wild puns, petty crimes or the singing of nonsense songs. Patients with mania don't seem to care about the rights of others and may over-react to people who interfere. Manic people may experience a flash of ideas or a great surge of creativity but are unable to put these qualities towards any use. Acute mania may also include hallucinations and delusions and the communication of these to other people. Mania is intense and may occur after a person has passed through hypomania or it might happen independently. At this stage there is often a loss of contact with reality, leading to psychosis. Hallucinations and delusions become pronounced and speech may become unintelligible. Patients in this stage of mania often demonstrate a lack of awareness of their surroundings.

In the DSM IV, mania is described as a distinct period of abnormally and persistently elevated, expansive or irritable mood, lasting at least one week or less if the patient is hospitalized. During the period of mood disturbance, three or more of the following exist and have been present to a significant degree:

1. Decreased need for sleep
2. Inflated self esteem or grandiosity

3. More talkative than usual or pressure to keep talking
4. Flight of ideas or racing thoughts
5. Distractibility
6. Increase in goal directed activity or agitation
7. Excessive involvement in pleasurable activities that have a high potential for painful consequences
8. The mood disturbance is severe enough to cause marked impairment in work-related functioning, social activities or to require hospitalization, to prevent harm to self or others
9. Psychotic features such as hallucinations or delusions
10. The symptoms are not directly caused by substance abuse, other medication or a medical condition

I have experienced all of these symptoms and still often lose sleep. My grandiose behaviour occurred in the hospital when I informed other patients that I was a messenger from God and also once in the community when I jumped over two rows of seats at a Toronto lecture conducted by neurologist Oliver Sacks. I ran up on the stage to give him a present and thought that in an audience of over two thousand people, I was the most important person. Needless to say, this was aberrant behaviour and I was pushed back into my seat by two security guards. Since I had met Dr. Sacks on two other occasions, I assumed that he would understand and even appreciate the gesture. Not so, I later found out.

Many of my friends and family members used to complain that I talked utter nonsense as I was getting ill, that I spoke too loudly and too quickly. Sometimes, I would speak in rhyme, but mostly, I just annoyed people. When I was severely manic, my thoughts jumped all over the place from one topic to another and eventually, I could not carry on a conversation. I was trying to make novel connections between unrelated ideas and I didn't make any sense. It didn't work. With all sorts of ideas and concepts racing through my head, I also started a large number of new projects including two books which I could not focus on well enough to finish. I also thought that I would start an interior design business with no credentials and I even tried to form a team of people to work for me from among the patients in the psychiatric ward of the hospital. Of course, all of this fell apart and no-one returned my calls when I made them.

By far the most dangerous behaviour I engaged in was extravagant spending. This started years ago before anyone suspected me of having bipolar disorder. I nearly ended up on the street because of the financial mess I got myself into and the web of lies I spun about my situation. As a result of my actions, positive relationships with others crumbled, but I felt that I had no control over what I was doing. Disinhibition seemed to be the theme of my behaviour. I even jumped out of an airplane (with a parachute) because I thought I was unstoppable. In addition, I acquired a love of speed and the activities that provided it such as barefoot waterskiing and driving fast. Despite the risk, the thrill of these activities intoxicated me, fed my mania and proved to me that I had no fear, not even healthy fear.

Mania is the most extreme of the bipolar symptoms and can be highly dangerous for several reasons. Firstly, manic patients enjoy the initial high of the condition and may feel like they have boundless energy and enthusiasm. These are positive feelings, but as the condition worsens, the patient can become seriously agitated, irrational, impulsive and uninhibited. This can lead to dangerous behaviour, perhaps even to suicide. In the initial stages of the illness, I started to speak too loudly, quickly and incoherently. I had grandiose ideas and thought that many scientific concepts were somehow miraculously connected. In addition, my memory seemed sharp at first and I felt like I could accomplish anything. Other changes in my thinking had a more gradual onset and took up to two years to develop. For example, my thoughts and attitudes about money and my ability to manage my finances progressively deteriorated over time as mania took hold. Over the last few years, before my bipolar illness erupted into full-blown mania, I increasingly spent money more recklessly. In addition, my speech became even faster and more pressured and eventually was unintelligible at the height of my last manic episode. Even my writing made no sense. I wrote everything frantically, thinking that I was creating unique relationships between concept and ideas. A sample from my little black book which I carried around with me in the hospital read like absolute nonsense: "children laughing someone knocking at my door sleep/

dream continuum, triangulation, cup runneth over, see world history problems". In this black book, I would also make extensive lists of things I wanted to buy, but of course, without the money to do so. The total cost of items ran into the tens of thousands, but I felt that some magical power within me would come up with the money. As a manic person, I had no concern for where my money would come from, or how I would pay my rent and bills. I felt fearless and did not comprehend the unpleasant and dangerous consequences of my actions. Impulsive behaviour and decision-making took over everything.

Eventually, I became impatient, agitated and intolerant of frustration. In the hospital, I ordered the other patients to take showers, demanded that they buy Avon products from me and threatened to sue my mother for one million dollars. Disturbed and disorganized, my thoughts became even more bizarre. The mania became increasingly more unpleasant and I at last realized that I was sick.

My diagnosis of bipolar I disorder consisted of a process of evaluations rather than a one-time event. By the time a clinician suspected that I might be a bipolar patient, I unknowingly had been exhibiting some symptoms for years, but was only being treated for anxiety, unipolar depression and Tourette's Syndrome. In retrospect, I can now recall periods of mood swings, erratic behaviour and poor judgment which punctuated the course of this illness. As I was escalating towards my first major episode of mania, In March of 2006, I was running out of money due to my wild spending. I sold all of my gold jewellery to a pawn shop for approximately five percent of its value in order to free up more money to spend unwisely.

As mania became a progressively more pronounced symptom of my illness, I became extravagant, irresponsible and uncontrollable with money. I maxed out credit cards using one card to pay off another. I couldn't stop myself from spending the maximum allowable amount at any given time and was so charged up about my purchases that I actually felt high. Unable to make even the minimum monthly payment on any of these cards, I simply ignored my debt, believing that somehow, the money would be available in the end.

A prominent memory of financial disaster involved an incident when I drove downtown to Toronto's most expensive shopping district on Bloor Street and charged five thousand dollars, the limit on my new Visa card, in less than one hour. I could feel the adrenalin pumping as I made my purchases and couldn't or refused to think about repaying this amount. On a young teacher's salary, I was buying Prada and Louis Vuitton like it was going out of style. Since I would not be able to make the minimum monthly payments on my credit cards, I took out a twenty thousand dollar line of credit to go on a trip to Africa where I bought a large collection of tribal art. After returning from that trip, I moved and borrowed even more money for that. Other people in my life could see that my behaviour was aberrant but I couldn't. My mind was churning so fast that I thought up all sorts of irresponsible schemes for finding money.

Eventually, I racked up such a huge debt that I couldn't even pay the interest on my credit cards and line of credit, and couldn't think clearly enough to find a way out. My attitude was foolhardy and audacious. I was unable to grasp the seriousness of the problem and didn't think there was anything wrong with me, and simply pushed the realities of my circumstances out of my mind and kept spending. My theory was, "Buy what you want and the money will follow. Lots of people have maxed out their credit cards", I rationalized. As far as I was concerned, I was just having fun, following my instincts and manic tendencies. However, in actuality, I created a highly stressful, risky situation for myself, not remotely adult-like in its nature. My friend Cathy and then my mother ended up bailing me out but I simply racked up more debt again.

Interestingly, the subject of my finances never came up with my psychiatrist during the period of time when I was being treated for anxiety, depression and Tourette's Syndrome. Certainly, I had complaints about tics, moodiness and sleep problems, but due to my lack of insight about my behaviour, I never thought to use therapy to discuss my money problems. Instead, I kept them hidden or else was in complete denial. Rather, I told my specialist about anger towards my mother which seemed to trigger symptoms of both depression and injudicious behaviour. I felt rejected by others as well and several times a year would seek out additional therapy to try to find a cause for my moodiness and depressive feelings. Relationship issues had become a source of distress for me, and other than the steady, close friends I had always had, I was making poor choices for new friends and boyfriends during that time. I thought that therapy would straighten me out and help me feel better but it didn't. Instead, I often confused therapists with articulate descriptions of mental ailments I was experiencing and rationalized my way in and out of therapy for years. No-one suspected bipolar disorder at the time. I overlooked my own contribution to my problems and placed the blame for my failures elsewhere.

Then, about six years ago, during a session with my Tourette's specialist, he told me point blank that he thought I might have bipolar disorder. With my background education in psychology, I'd certainly heard of this condition, but I asked the psychiatrist for an explanation of his suspicion. He informed me that I had rapid, pressured speech and that my thoughts were flighty and somewhat nonsensical. Vehemently, I disagreed with all of this and in fact, we didn't discuss any other bipolar symptoms at that time such as the squandering of money. He didn't even use the term manic to describe me. Therefore, I didn't think my condition (if in fact I had it) was that serious and ignored his diagnosis.

Weeks after that session, I booked myself on a trip to New York City for five days and went there with less than one hundred dollars in my wallet. I checked into a luxury boutique hotel on the upper east side of Manhatten and had no idea how I would pay even a small portion of that bill or survive for the duration of my stay. At the end of the first day, I was penniless and had no money for food, transportation or anything else. But, I was excited and I was there to shop! So, that first night, when the money was gone, I began calling friends and family back home with all sorts of stories about how I had lost my money and would they please wire me some. Highly manipulative, I promised to pay everyone back soon. I conjured up all sorts of excuses about how I'd lost my money and managed to get more than ten people to send me hundreds of dollars. I quickly spent all of the money with wild abandon on costume jewellery and over thirty bottles of perfume. Up and down Madison and Fifth Avenue I ran, filled with adrenalin, spending money that wasn't mine to spend. The fact that I would have to pay people back never crossed my mind. An acquaintance of mine in New York even paid my hotel bill for me, which was well over a thousand dollars.

By the time I got back from New York with all the junk I had purchased, I owed money to more than fifteen people from this trip alone. Of course, I still had my credit card debt, overdraft protection and line of credit to deal with as well. I just didn't seem to be able to think about the consequences of my actions, but in retrospect, the only person I was fooling was myself.

When I next saw my Tourette's specialist and told him about New York, a bright red flag went up in his mind and he essentially insisted that I had bipolar disorder, despite my lengthy rationalization of my recent spending. I refused to think that I had a mental illness. I knew only that I'd had depression and anxiety in the past and was already on maintenance medication for those symptoms. Surely, nothing else was wrong with me!

Sceptical and wanting a second opinion, I asked for a referral to a neurologist, certain that the diagnosis of bipolar disorder would be dropped. I assured my psychiatrist that I didn't have the illness but perhaps had something structural that was wrong with my brain. However, I did begin to do some research (as is my nature) about bipolar disorder and especially about the treatment and medication, and I did learn some new terms and what they meant. As it turned out, the neurologist agreed with my Tourette's psychiatrist that I had bipolar II disorder and he pointed out some of the same symptoms to me – namely, rapid, pressured speech, agitation and confrontational behaviour. He felt that I was hypomanic.

Still, I denied the diagnosis. "What am I supposed to be feeling"? I thought. Then a few weeks later, without medication for bipolar disorder, I started to get into even more financial trouble even though I still believed there was nothing wrong with me. For example, no-one had informed me that the nature of my irresponsible spending was actually a manic symptom of the disorder. At any rate, it wasn't long before my overall behaviour was getting quite unusual. I wasn't sleeping and my mind was racing.

Hypomania and Bipolar II Disorder

In bipolar disorder, hypomania, a less severe symptom than mania may occur prior to mania or it may exist independently. The DSM IV describes hypomania as a distinct period of persistently elevated, expansive or irritable mood, lasting at least four days that is clearly different from the usual non-depressed mood. Three or more of the following have persisted (four if the mood is only irritable) and have been present to a significant degree:

1. Inflated self esteem or grandiosity
2. More talkative than usual or pressured speech
3. Decreased need for sleep
4. Flighty or racing thoughts
5. Distractibility
6. Increase in goal directed activity or agitation
7. Excessive involvement in pleasurable activities that have a high potential for painful consequence

Hypomanic episodes are associated with a definite change in functioning that is uncharacteristic of the person when not symptomatic. Changes in mood and functioning are observable by others but the hypomanic episode is not severe enough to cause marked impairment in social or work-related functioning, or to require hospitalization and there is no psychosis. Hypomania is not caused by a substance or general medical condition. If patients have at least one episode of depression and one episode of hypomania, then bipolar II disorder is diagnosed.

Initially, while still seeing my Tourette's specialist, I was diagnosed with bipolar II disorder and had not had an episode of full mania yet, but in retrospect there were quite a number of hypomanic episodes I had experienced since 1988. I'd also had several depressions, but during those years, no-one was completely certain about what was causing the hypomania. I can recall the sense of always being on the go, constantly writing, talking on the phone and staying up all night reading. Intense arguments with my boyfriend and later my landlady marked my behaviour. In addition, I had conflicts with my principal at work and was easily overwhelmed with anger toward my mother. However, at other times, I felt so good and productive that I relished the feeling. At these times, I was skilled at word play, had boundless energy for sports, and stayed up partying with friends from my waterskiing crowd until early morning hours. Without a doubt, however, my judgment was clouded. I would drive home from the lake after drinking with friends or at other times would drive too fast. However, when I was hypomanic, I was highly creative, inventing unique lesson plans for my students and feeling much more at ease socially. The problem was, I felt so good that I didn't seek treatment while in this state. Instead, I enjoyed the adrenalin, energy, creativity, happiness and productivity. My view was that this mood of hypomania was part of Tourette's Syndrome and that was that. However, other people had a hard time figuring me out during episodes of hypomania. I would become quite selfish and sometimes would disregard the rights of others.

Overall, hypomania was confusing to me, partly because it was so inconsistent and because I couldn't figure out where the high moods came from. I'd suddenly be hurled into a world of new possibilities and ideas and a greater ability to work. I felt, "I must record anything and everything", and I made lists and notes and thought that everything that happened to me was worthwhile and purposeful.

So, for twenty years, states of hypomania felt normal to me. Admittedly, there are some parts of that state that I miss – especially the high levels of creativity and sociability. What I have learned, however, is that discipline (which is much easier to enlist now that I am medicated) helps to develop creativity and more consistent productivity. I have also learned to have consistently positive relationships with people and that counts a great deal.

Bipolar Depression

Pain, torture, loss, devastation, hopelessness, worthlessness – I have no difficulty recalling the depressions I have experienced. I felt like dying, like being in hell with no way out. Also, my depressions lasted much longer than my manic or hypomanic states and punctuated my life for over twenty years.

The DSM IV description of depression includes at least five of the following symptoms present during the same two-week period and indicating a change from previous functioning:

1. Depressed mood observable by self or others
2. Markedly diminished pleasure in activities
3. Significant weight loss or weight gain
4. Insomnia or hypersomnia
5. Psychomotor agitation or slowing
6. Fatigue or loss of energy
7. Feelings of worthlessness or excessive guilt
8. Distractibility or indecisiveness

9. Recurrent thoughts of death, suicidal ideation, plans or attempts

Most people are familiar with some of the symptoms of depression and there has been a proliferation of research pertaining to it and its treatment. Beyond ordinary sadness, depression is characterized by extremely low mood and physical and mental slowing. Symptoms such as agitation, panic, uneasiness or apprehension may also appear, and did in my case. In its most severe form, depression can involve delusions of worthlessness. I felt this way for nearly a year, and essentially lost hope. The illness can cause bodily changes such as weight gain or weight loss as well. I was so ill that for a while, I was unable to swallow food – it would make me feel sick. As a result, I lost so much weight that at nearly six feet tall, I had to wear clothes in children's sizes. At least I did not become psychotic, but this can happen, where a person my hallucinate voices belittling himself or herself and suicide can become a real threat.

There are three levels of severity in depression. The mildest form is called simple depression. Its features include a general slowing of functioning associated with a loss of enthusiasm for physical and mental activity. A person may feel a sense of numbness or a void within herself. Every task including eating and washing seems too difficult to complete and each minute of the day feels very heavy and sad. Fortunately, at this stage, a person has not yet lost logical thinking abilities and there is rarely an occurrence of hallucinations or delusions. Everyone feels the blues sometimes but when depressive episodes recur without any connection to real situations, the patient is diagnosed with simple depression.

Acute depression is more severe. For example, physical and motor movements become severely retarded, activity level drops sharply, avoidance of social contact prevails and feelings of guilt my also exist. At this stage, thoughts of suicide become common and sleep is extremely difficult. The patient feels helpless, hopeless and indifferent and may experience delusional beliefs. My first depressive episode reached this stage and I only avoided hospitalization by a small margin.

Depressive stupor is the most pronounced form of depression. With few exceptions, patients are totally inactive and socially unresponsive. They often refuse to eat, lose control of bodily functions and usually need hospitalization in order to obtain intravenous feeding and catheterization. Fortunately, a newer form of electro shock therapy can reduce the experience of depressive stupor. In my experience, I have never reached this stage of depression but I am aware that it could be a possibility if I did not take my medication.

In bipolar disorder, depressive episodes are easier and more familiar to diagnose and easier for patients to describe than are manic episodes. Individuals in depression who can't recover from intense gloom and despair however, may be preoccupied with the need to blame themselves for symptoms or be responsible for them. For example, twenty years ago, I thought that my actions at the end of my marriage were responsible for my depression. I did not realize that the condition was clinical and caused by a mental illness. I felt worthless, unloved and without purpose and was regularly weepy and uncomfortable with myself. Loneliness and a sense of loss put me out of touch with people. I would call others to talk about my feelings but it wouldn't help. Highly anxious that this condition would never leave, I couldn't pay attention to or focus on anything and could hardly get out of bed. When I did get up, I would wander despondently around my apartment. I thought, "Is this all there is?" about life. Without energy, I could not even make myself something to eat. Household tasks went by the wayside and my home became a chaotic nightmare. I couldn't decide what to do so I just stayed in bed for days. Sleep came too little or too late. I became lazy, indifferent and avoidant. The only thing I could do was ruminate about my illness. My life felt meaningless.

I was first diagnosed with depression in 1988 during the breakdown and termination of my marriage. The experience was in many ways the opposite of the acute mania I suffered recently, but was just as devastating. It has taken many years to discover that my depression was part of the broader spectrum of bipolar disorder and it is only after much reflection, research and discussion with friends, family and professionals that I finally understand it better.

Panic attacks were my first symptom of depression. Out of nowhere came shortness of breath, chest pain and nausea. I felt like I was losing control of my body and I had an enormous sense of fear. I could not speak or think clearly or control my rapid, shallow breathing. I tried to practise deep breathing to calm myself down but to no avail. These panic feelings lasted for hours and when the symptoms finally subsided, I was exhausted. It felt like I had a heart attack and needed to get to a doctor. At the time, I didn't realize that my symptoms were related to a mental condition as opposed to a physical one. At my doctor's office, I was given an ECG, had my blood pressure and pulse taken, underwent a chest X-Ray and had blood tests. Everything appeared to be normal. I didn't understand.

Over the next few weeks the panic attacks occurred closer and closer together. My marriage was concurrently falling apart and I realized eventually that I was experiencing a severe form of anxiety over the events of my life. At the same time, I was applying to the public school board as a teacher for the first time. During interviews, I mustered as much energy as I could in order to appear normal, although I felt anything but. Somehow, I secured a position as a special education teacher of children with psychiatric and behavioural difficulties. Little did I know that these children were in better shape than I was.

By the time I started my new job, my panic attacks became so severe that I could barely function at all. I was contemplating the fact that if I couldn't straighten myself out, I would have no home, no marriage and no employment. The attacks were now lasting for five or six hours at a time, after which I was completely depleted.

Finally, I sought emergency psychiatric help and was referred to a psychiatrist whose office was close to my home. By the time I had my first appointment with her, I was in so much despair and anguish that I thought my symptoms would kill me if I didn't get help.

I had so little control of my mind and body at that time that I honestly felt like I was dying.

After struggling through an initial assessment with the psychiatrist, I was informed that I had a severe anxiety disorder and would need to be on medication. The psychiatrist also wanted to admit me to the hospital but I vehemently refused. Anything but that, I thought. To me a hospital stay would mean that I had lost myself and I knew that I had to fight to hang on to the last vestiges of sanity.

In the midst of all this turmoil, I moved out of the matrimonial home and into a temporary arrangement in the home of my mother's friend in Toronto. I also took a specialist course in special education which I passed with high honours. My psychiatrist prescribed a low dosage of an antidepressant at this time and gradually increased it but it was not helping. I was in deep despair and started to experience even more symptoms of depression. Sleeping and eating were virtually impossible. It was difficult to fall asleep and when I did at times drift off, I would awaken at three or four a.m. and immediately start to panic.

After several days of this, I was so distraught that I telephoned my psychiatrist at her home and reported that I was worried about becoming suicidal. She was very alarmed and advised me to increase the dose of my medication markedly. She explained that I would experience some side effects such as low blood pressure, dizziness, sedation and dry mouth. I would have to get up very slowly in the morning to avoid fainting. In addition to the antidepressant, I was given an anti-panic medication to take when needed. However, for six or seven weeks, my depressive symptoms were unrelenting, and the medication didn't seem to help. I was advised not to make any major life changes during this time as they would likely cause undue stress. For me however, my indecision about my marriage was triggering my illness. If I couldn't make a decision, I thought, then I might as well be dead.

By the time I had done some research, I started to become very familiar with some of the other classic symptoms of depression. I did not become psychotic or have delusions and hallucinations, but I completely lost the ability to experience pleasure in any activity. It was exhausting just to think about what I had to do each minute just to get by. I would become very weepy after panic attacks and my thought processes slowed down significantly. Unable to solve even simple problems or complete simple tasks like making a sandwich, I plummeted into even deeper depression. Somehow, I taught children through all of this but I was miserable.

Once I was in the depths of despair, I never thought I would get any better and was close to giving up. My future looked bleak and I could think of no reason for my existence. Everything seemed gray and black and meaningless. I felt alienated from my surroundings and from the people I usually counted on. A sense of unreality permeated my existence and I felt like I was observing myself through a glass wall. Because my cognitive abilities had diminished so much, I found it extremely difficult to plan lessons for my students. Every time I tried to focus or think, I would end up having a panic attack, feeling completely paralyzed, an empty vessel with nothing to offer. I had no ideas, no creativity and no motivation to do anything. To me, most tasks seemed meaningless and pointless and so I would not or could not perform.

Emotionally, there were other components of depression that I experienced. The perpetual anxiety I was feeling drove me toward ruminating behaviour and as I went over and over the same events in my life, or the same readings about depression, it was never enough. I had little concentration and was confused by it all, unable to feel, think or care. In addition, since anxiety was a major element of my depression, I acquired many irrational fears such as a fear of poverty and of not being able to cope if I lived alone. I worried that I would lose all my friends and that my family would reject me. Normally attentive to my appearance, I demonstrated poor self care as the symptoms became more pervasive. I wore baggy old clothes, no make-up and often didn't even bother with a coat or gloves in the middle of winter. I became self-accusatory and continued to demonstrate self-deprecating thoughts and behaviours.

Physically, there were a number of changes in my countenance. I became gaunt and sallow in complexion, and rapidly lost a lot of weight. My gait was slow and awkward and I moved lethargically. My face looked drawn after months of not being able to smile, my posture was poor and I had dark circles under my eyes. I had no energy and had to sit or lie down most of the time. However, this was not restful. On the contrary, I was restless and could never seem to shift into a comfortable position. My muscles ached from lack of use. Two more months passed before I was able to make any improvements.

Eventually, after approximately ten weeks of therapy and medical treatment, I started to experience periods of calm and lucid thinking. The antidepressant medication was beginning to take effect and the frequency of my panic attacks started to diminish. I began to eat a little bit and was slightly more able to complete tasks.

Then on one November morning, as I was driving to work, I experienced a kind of epiphany. It had been a cold, bleak and rainy month. Quite suddenly, the clouds above me parted, allowing the sun to shine through. At that moment, I knew I would leave my marriage and begin the journey to recovery.

It should be noted that it was the combination of therapy, medication and thus improved symptomology that facilitated my recovery. When I twice tried to wean myself off the medication, I experienced relapses and so have continued to take antidepressant medication for the last twenty years under the supervision of a psychiatrist. At that time, on some level, I knew that I had a mental illness and yet there were still questions I had about why I didn't recover fully and needed to stay on medication. No-one suspected bipolar disorder.

Bipolar Disorder – Mixed Episode

I have never been diagnosed with mixed episodes of bipolar disorder, but I do recall depressive episodes several times per year that were serious enough for me to seek therapy, even though I was already on medication. Because I lacked insight about my own hypomania and wasn't diagnosed with bipolar disorder at the time, I cannot recall whether or not I had mixed episodes as opposed to distinct periods of hypomanic and depressive symptoms.

A mixed episode occurs when an individual experiences mania and depression concurrently for at least one week. According to the DSM IV, the episode is severe enough to cause marked impairment in occupational functioning, social activities and relationships with others. It may necessitate hospitalization to prevent harm to oneself or others and there may be psychosis. A mixed episode is not due to the direct effects of a substance or a general medical condition.

Patients who suffer mania and depression at the same time may be restless and distractible, involved in senseless and frenetic activity and may feel hopeless at the same time. Speech and behaviour may be aberrant and disorderly but yet expressionless. There may possibly be a tendency toward uninhibited violent behaviour like punching walls or throwing things.

Overall, mixed states may include euphoria, depression, irritability, hostility, disorientation, distractibility, grandiosity, decreased or increased sexuality, increased substance abuse, possible delusions, hallucinations, impulsive spending, anxiety and suicidal ideation or behaviour.

A dear and brilliant friend of mine experiences mixed episodes which are highly confusing to him and others. These episodes make his life highly chaotic and unpredictable at times and he is constantly looking for ways to experience inner peace. Mixed episodes are exhausting and often tragic.

Cyclothymia

Cyclothymia means the rapid cycling of manic and depressive episodes of bipolar disorder. For example, within days, patients may demonstrate manic or hypomanic behaviour such as euphoria, hyperactivity, over-talkativeness and occasionally hallucinations or delusions. A person's thoughts may be unfocussed, shallow, aimless or incoherent. Then within a few hours or days, there may be a switch to depression and the patient may become sullen, lethargic and possibly psychotic or even suicidal. People may feel like they are switching from one personality to another giving them a Jekyl and Hyde feeling.

Although I am not cyclothymic, I have in my teaching career, taught two students who fit this profile. One was a young boy of seven who would often erupt into silly and giddy laughter without a trigger and would stay this way for hours. Following this behaviour, he would become morose, tearful and withdrawn, and would hide under a table or under his desk. He would make self deprecating comments and would attempt to destroy his good work, which troubled the other students. Occasionally, he would escalate into a rage, throwing objects or attacking his peers. When Jay was not in an episode, he was a sweet, co-operative, articulate child who took pride in his achievements and liked to please me as his teacher. He would often carry things for me, even though he was a tiny boy or complete little chores around the classroom. It was heartbreaking to witness him struggle with cyclothymia and I learned how to deal with him but Jay didn't understand what was happening to him and he would seek me out to comfort him.

Jay's entire countenance would change as he passed through his episodes. When he was manic, his eyes were wild and his body was tense. He had an almost evil look about him. When he switched to a depressive mood, his face became drawn and pale, and he would choose an object to stare at for hours. Sadly, many of the other teachers and even the child-care workers in my classroom, thought he was demonstrating these behaviours to get attention. The lack of insight and compassion he got from others was inexcusable and frustrated me to no end. I nearly lost my job insisting that he have a psychiatric assessment, but this was nearly twenty years ago when knowledge about bipolar disorder in children was limited.

Unfortunately, Jay's family decided to move before the school year ended and I never got to see the psychiatric report. Curious, I tracked down the family eleven years later and learned that he had bipolar disorder (his family called it manic depression at the time). At that point in his life, the illness had really taken hold of him. When he was a teenager, he had substance abuse problems, had committed several crimes (assault and drug related) and had become a loner. I never found out exactly how he was treated but he was a child of quarrelling, uneducated parents and was obviously still having much difficulty coping.

Anna, an older student of mine (age thirteen) was more fortunate in getting a diagnosis of cyclothymia and she has to this day responded well to medication and therapy. By the time Anna was my student, more was known about bipolar disorder but of course, I didn't know that I had it myself. At any rate, this young lady exhibited some unusual behaviours in class which reflected her condition. When she was episodic, she too started with hypomania. It would usually begin with inappropriate laughing and a regression to childlike behaviours such as sucking her thumb or throwing tantrums. She was a big girl, so everyone noticed. At these times, she was unable to work or follow classroom rules and I had to put a lot of structure in place in order to contain her. She became combative and defiant and she would get stuck in this state for hours.

Then suddenly, there would be a switch to a sullen and tearful mood. Anna would crawl under a table and rock back and forth sometimes fidgeting with a children's toy. She became unresponsive and would not react to either positive discipline or encouragement. Eventually however, she would pull out of this state and demonstrate remorse for her negative behaviour even though she didn't understand it. When questioned, Anna never wanted to talk about these episodes because they frightened her. She was insightful in some ways however. After episodes had passed, she would throw herself into her work and would accomplish some excellent results. She would be able to discuss her strengths and needs and would be quite skillful at assisting the younger students when she had completed her own assignments.

By the time she was fourteen, Anna had been placed on medication for bipolar disorder and was doing much better. She was able to do volunteer work in the summer and eventually became more age appropriate in her overall behaviour. It was interesting that even though her psychiatrist had her on a mood stabilizer and an antidepressant, the words "bipolar disorder" were not initially explained to her family. I am no longer in contact with this family but her parents are proactive, and I can only hope that she will continue to respond to treatment and will gain some awareness of her illness.

The DSM IV describes cyclothymic patients as suffering from chronic symptoms of mood disorder fluctuating between hypomania and simple depression. These individuals, however, do not experience full-blown psychotic mania or major depression. During a two year period (one year for children and adolescents) patients are symptom free for no longer than two months. After that time, either a manic, depressive or mixed episode may occur when either bipolar I disorder or bipolar II disorder would be diagnosed. Either way, cyclothymia is not diagnosed unless there is significant impairment in social, job-related or other areas of functioning and the symptoms cause marked distress.

Regardless of what phase of the disorder cyclothymic patients are in, they are in a constant battle with their surroundings, having lost their emotional balance. In addition, others who are around the patient might feel very confused about what he or she is dealing with. Before I learned about my own bipolar disorder, it certainly was confusing watching the children I taught suffer so much and I wish they could have found relief sooner.

Diagnostic Difficulties

The diagnosis of bipolar disorder can be a complicated process and at times, major depression is diagnosed instead. This happens because many patients fail to recognize manic or hypomanic symptoms in themselves and therefore, because of this lack of insight, can't report them. Initially, an incorrect diagnosis happened in my case. Over twenty years ago, I was diagnosed with major depression, but looking back, I can certainly recall and identify situations where I was hypomanic, made huge judgment errors and was extravagant with money. At the time, I had no real explanations for these impulsive behaviours and didn't think to talk about them with a psychiatrist.

Another difficulty in diagnostics for this disorder is that because patients who are hypomanic report feeling normal or really good, doctors must rely on observers such as family, friends and colleagues as well as their own observations to come up with a diagnosis. For example, once the diagnostic process got underway with me, it took well over two years to make it clear to me that I was bipolar, since so many other people had to be consulted, in order to report their observations. Until I had a psychotic manic episode, I did not agree with my diagnosis or co-operate with treatment. Right through the duration of my first hospital stay, I denied it and it wasn't until I was psychotic and manic, and when my family was interviewed in depth that my diagnosis was confirmed and effective treatment began.

There are other patient factors leading to misdiagnosis including memory impairment in either depression or mania. Approximately one year prior to my diagnosis, I started having short-term memory problems and was very aware and concerned about this symptom but not of others. As a result, I saw a neurologist instead of a psychiatrist and of course, my performance on all tests was normal.

Clinical factors can also present problems in the diagnosis of bipolar disorder. For example, much research has confirmed that there is a significant relationship between a family member's mental health and the mental health of the patient. Therefore, if family members are not included in the assessment, an accurate diagnosis of bipolar disorder might be missed. My assessment involved soliciting a family history from me and two separate interviews with members of my family. My doctors discovered that indeed there was a significant psychiatric history in my family which included depression, alcohol abuse and hypomania. This knowledge was used to aid in the confirmation of my diagnosis.

A limited knowledge of understanding of manic symptoms may also present problems in diagnosis. This played out in my case in a number of ways. First of all, I didn't report mania in myself as a particular mood, but rather as some bizarre mental illness that included memory loss, increased creativity, poor judgment and shoplifting. These symptoms are not listed in the

DSM IV and therefore, I confused clinicians as well as myself.

Secondly, the nature of my diagnosis of bipolar disorder was made too instinctively. Three specialists suggested that I had bipolar II disorder because of forced speech and sleeping problems. However, it wasn't until my second hospitalization that a more comprehensive, scientific method of diagnosis was used to confirm bipolar I disorder.

Thirdly, it was much easier to diagnose unipolar depression than it was to diagnose bipolar disorder. Symptoms of depression are clearly understood by doctors and often by patients and many effective treatments are known. Twenty-one years ago, my psychiatrist at the time diagnosed depression expediently and both of us agreed on the symptoms. Therefore, medication was prescribed at once. However, it did not occur to this specialist to assess me for anything else at the time, as less was known about bipolar disorder then.

A fourth significant problem in the diagnosis of bipolar disorder is that depressive episodes often last much longer than briefer hypomanic or manic episodes. My first bout of depression diagnosed in 1988 lasted for one full year. My longest manic episode lasted for two weeks prior to intervention and other hypomanic episodes were even shorter. Therefore, the chances of identifying my hypomanic states were slim compared to identifying the depression.

In order for the diagnosis of bipolar disorder to be precise, there are certain techniques which should be avoided. Surveys or self-rating scales can be inaccurate due to a patient's instability, poor judgment, weak thinking skills, distractibility and denial. Therefore, a diagnosis must be made on the basis of observation such as: the patient has racing thoughts, talks too much, makes unrealistic plans, spends money recklessly and is irritable.

Sometimes, professional or book descriptions of bipolar disorder make it look like it's not that difficult to diagnose and yet it is. According to Miclowitz (2002), there is an average of eight years between the onset of bipolar disorder and its first diagnosis. The illness looks like it could be many things depending on a person's perspective. In addition, diagnosis can be difficult because symptoms can change between one person and the next and often change within one person between one episode and the next. For example, a patient may suffer one part of the disorder such as depression and then symptoms may remain dormant for years.

Finally, comorbid conditions can add to confusion on the part of the patient and the clinicians. I suffered from Tourette's Syndrome and severe insomnia during the years prior to my diagnosis of bipolar disorder and it was difficult for specialists to determine what symptoms went with what illness. As a result, I continued to exasperate doctors and wear out my family and friends. Eventually, once I was hospitalized in November of 2006 and was more co-operative, a firm diagnosis was reached and targeted treatment began.

Trends and Causes of Bipolar Disorder

There are some startling trends to uncover when studying how bipolar disorder affects the lives of patients. Current estimates are that close to three percent of the population have the illness. Hornbacher (2008) reveals some other statistics that are shocking as well. According to his research, the life expectancy of adults with a serious mental illness is twenty-five years shorter than that of those without. He also reveals that in particular, twenty-five percent of bipolar patients have attempted suicide and fifteen to twenty percent of those individuals have actually ended their lives. In addition, the average age of onset for bipolar disorder is twenty-three although the average age for correct diagnosis is much older likely due to diagnostic difficulties. In fact, the number of bipolar patients who have been misdiagnosed at least once is between seventy and seventy-five percent. It is estimated that about half of bipolar patients don't seek or receive treatment at all. In addition, the divorce rate for bipolar patients in their first marriage is three and one half times higher than the rate of divorce in the general population. Finally, patients who go off their medication are the most likely to relapse.

These statistics (and more are provided in Hornbacher's work) point to a need for rigorous research and refinement of diagnostic techniques as well as a need for increased awareness in the general population about bipolar disorder.

Causes of Bipolar Disorder

When I first accepted the fact that I had bipolar disorder, my next question was, "How did I get this?" Fortunately, new research has led to a greater understanding of the illness and its etiology.

Bipolar disorder tends to run in families. Research has hypothesized that there is a genetic component as well as a biological one. However, these components aren't fully understood and the methodology of the research may be unclear. Nevertheless, one theory is that bipolar disorder is caused by deficiencies in the biochemistry and physiology of the brain and nervous system. For example, adrenalin is often released during a stress response. If it is too high, mania may be the result and if it is too low, depression may occur. In addition, neurotransmitters such as dopamine, serotonin and norepinephrine all play a part in the manifestation of the illness, and many of the medications act on these neurotransmitters, putting the brain's biology back into balance. However, more research is needed to uncover exactly how these medications work and in what part of the brain they operate. According to Burgess (2006), there appear to be several areas of the brain that are involved in the manifestation of bipolar disorder including the amygdala, frontal lobe, temporal lobe and hippocampus. Burgess also postulates that bipolar patients lose brain cells more rapidly than those without the disorder.

Much research has been aimed at genetic causes for bipolar disorder. Studies have shown that there is a greater likelihood for bipolar disorder to occur in the children of bipolar parents. For example, I recall my father having explosive rages, bouts of depression and trouble with alcohol when I was younger. Certainly, his depression lasted for the rest of his life once he was diagnosed but he was resistant to treatment because he didn't cope well with the side effects of the medication and he refused psychotherapy because he felt superior to his clinicians. Indeed, he was a highly intelligent man but became somewhat of a loner in later life and therefore wouldn't or couldn't solicit support from others. As a result, his mood was unstable from his mid forties until he passed away about twenty years later.

I remember depression and rage on my mother's side of the family as well. As I was growing up, my mother often seemed angry, depressed and obsessive and was unable to use strategies to resolve these feelings. She lacked a sense of humour at the time and could be verbally and passively aggressive towards my father and me. Fortunately, she has now become more aware of how her behaviour affects others and is coping much better now. Her mother, (my grandmother), was an alcoholic and committed suicide so that she would not have to die a slow death in a nursing home. There are other mental health issues in more distant relatives which are highly uncomfortable to discuss and potentially damaging to various family members, so I will conclude by saying that there is a history of psychiatric illness on both sides of my family which likely is related to my bipolar disorder. Of course there were some good times growing up as a young child, but mostly, I remember the sadness, tension, fear and anger, especially during my later childhood and adolescent years. It should be noted that my perceptions at that time may indicate that I was possibly mildly depressed.

Most of the research suggests that bipolar disorder is considered to be a chemical and genetic disorder that can be triggered by environmental factors. In my case, various traumas were always present, whether I was in depression or mania. My first full-blown bipolar episode, which was depression, occurred as my marriage crumbled in 1988 and it was the first time I was medicated for a mental illness. Subsequent depressions arose at critical points during a very rocky relationship I pursued after my marriage ended. Clearly, I was not skilled at choosing appropriate life partners, yet unfortunately, each of these relationships took up seven years of my life. However, as I matured and became stronger, with the help of therapy and medication, I was able to terminate these unhealthy relationships and move on more positively with my life.

If only it had been as easy as all that. In the years that followed, I had experiences at work or traumatic confrontations with my mother that would precipitate episodes. Eventually, since I was not medicated for bipolar disorder, these episodes became more bizarre and manic in nature.

Then all hell broke loose. As I escalated into mania back in 2006, I made another poor decision to take in a young tenant because I needed the extra money. Not only did this young man have bipolar disorder as I did, but he was also an alcoholic, drug addict and victim of borderline personality disorder, and he became violent. After threatening my life, he was incarcerated for three months but I continued to live in fear of him.

Soon after, a psychotic manic episode ensued and I was back in the hospital again.

The environmental triggers I have described here provoked episodes of mania or depression although my predisposition towards bipolar disorder was already apparent. Triggers that other patients may experience could include hormones, street drugs, sleep deprivation, stress, illness or injury to name a few.

In summary, the causes of bipolar disorder are multifaceted, involving neurotransmitters, genetics and environmental triggers. Hopefully, continued research will unmask the mysteries of the illness and lead to discoveries which will bring forth profound changes for patients and their families and loved ones.

Chapter 5
Outcomes of Bipolar Disorder

Bipolar disorder can be dangerous. Left untreated, it can ruin lives, destroy relationships and even end in suicide. The illness includes contrasting episodes of various lengths and levels of severity which profoundly affect thoughts, feelings and behaviours.

At approximately the same time that my marriage in my twenties began to fall apart, I started to experience depressive episodes so severe that I thought I would die from the physical symptoms (for example, severe chest pain and rapid heart rate). Prior to the experience of clinical symptoms, I felt some mild depression for about six months and attributed it to disillusionment with my marriage. I'm still not sure which was the chicken or the egg but in the end, I terminated my marriage and with the help of medication got well again – at least for a while. Over the next fifteen years or so, I had some emotional fall-outs with my mother that affected me deeply and I periodically experienced more fleeting but nonetheless recurring symptoms of depression. Looking back, I still cannot determine which came first – the depression or the relationship difficulties. I do know now that since I've been treated for bipolar disorder, my relationship with my mother has healed and that is one of the single most important elements of my wellness.

Prior to treatment, I certainly sabotaged other relationships during hypomanic and manic states. The bottom line is that some family and friends have not forgiven me for my bipolar behaviour, but fortunately, most of the important people in my life have taken an interest in my welfare and I simply have to move on at this point. I think I have done as much damage control as possible. I am now much healthier in the decisions that I make and the relationships that I keep and in the past three years have felt more stable than I've ever felt in my life.

One of the most devastating outcomes I experienced with bipolar disorder was financial ruin. For eighteen years (after I was first diagnosed with depression), I spent money recklessly, as an impulsive and compulsive shopper – a girl who liked nice things. I always felt that the money would come from somewhere and for a while, it did. Eventually and repeatedly, I landed myself in huge debt and lost the trust of everyone when it came to money matters. I ended up with a lot of stuff (more than anyone could possibly need), a lot of stress and came very close to losing my home (having spent my rent money), and living on the street. Very fortunately for me, I had people who helped me get in touch with a credit counsellor once I was in treatment and I have successfully paid off my debt to a total of twenty-six creditors. I still enjoy window shopping but I don't want any more stuff and am learning to give things away. My only weakness is books, and that runs in the family!

For just over four years, I have been in treatment and overall, it feels much better to be in control of my life and to behave consistently. I am now debt free for the first time in over twenty years and know that I will be able to stay that way, since I have learned how to plan and follow a budget. When I look back over those troublesome times, I realize now that I had put myself in an extremely dangerous position and got help with no time to spare. Medication and therapy have enabled me to control the hypomania and mania which led to spending sprees. I consider myself to be very fortunate.

Others are not so lucky. There have been patients who have squandered all of their family's savings and who have lost everything because their illness went untreated. I was fortunate that my bipolar disorder was diagnosed just in time before I completely ruined myself financially and I would say that positive outcomes of this illness depend on getting the correct diagnosis and treatment on time.

As it stands, I'm still greatly embarrassed by my past financial indiscretion and by the fact that I have to re-establish the trust of others when it comes to money and my credit rating. Most people my age have been able to build up savings and investments, whereas I am just now, in my late forties, starting from scratch. The good thing is that I am now highly motivated, have control over my spending behaviour and have the support of friends and family who have taken the time to get to know this illness and its effects.

People ask me whether I would ever consider getting married again. Bipolar disorder is associated with high divorce rates and decreased frequency of marriage. According to Redfield-Jamison (2007), bipolar individuals may tend to marry someone who has an affective illness. A benefit may be that there is a common understanding between partners; however there is also a likelihood that the marriage and family life will be unstable. I divorced in the middle of a depressive episode over twenty years ago and have not yet remarried. I often wonder whether divorce would have been the outcome had I been diagnosed correctly years ago. Who knows! I did as much research about mental illness and symptoms as any individual could be expected to do.

In addition to the destruction of relationships and the mismanagement of money, the loss of a job or one's sense of status is another possible outcome of bipolar disorder. This was a very real concern for me. As my illness worsened, I had much difficulty remaining stable in my teaching position. Since I was a special education teacher, there was not much room for error. Yet, I progressively suffered more short-term memory loss as well as alternating moods. My ability to sleep also worsened and I started to miss too much work. At the time, I had an unsupportive bully of a principal who contributed a great deal of stress to an already difficult situation. Eventually, the illness overwhelmed me and I had to leave teaching and go on long-term disability support.

In order to stay well now, I have to keep negative stress to a minimum and sleep when I can. However, I still suffer from extreme insomnia. Structure in my day is very important but I have had to accept that because of bipolar disorder, I cannot manage my job anymore. Others find that after treatment has progressed, they can go back to work after episodes subside and maintain their employment status. I have chosen to write because the hours I work don't affect anyone else and writing gives me a sense of purpose.

Psychosis

What is happening to me? Why are these voices banging inside my head? What will people think of me? God, make it stop!

Psychosis is a term used to describe a patient's mental state when he/she is out of touch with reality. It is a medical condition that exists because of a dysfunction in the brain. People suffering from psychosis have trouble separating false experiences from real ones and may demonstrate strange or risky behaviour without being aware of it. The symptoms of psychosis make it difficult for patients to conduct daily activities. In a psychotic episode, individuals may experience hallucinations and/or delusions which are very real for the patient. Psychosis is treatable and may or may not be a symptom of bipolar disorder. It is important for individuals experiencing it to seek help as the condition is highly troubling and interferes with life. People with psychosis usually have serious problems such as being unable to work or participate in social activities. They may also suffer confused thinking and speech. Prior to my last hospital stay, I experienced a psychotic episode which included hallucinations and delusions. Each of these is discussed below.

Hallucinations

Many famous creative and artistic scholars have reported hallucinations in their lives, including Socrates, Carl Jung, Winston Churchill, Andy Warhol, Galileo, Pythagorus and Gandhi. A hallucination is a sensory experience for which there is no external stimuli. It is not imagined, conjured up or created by a person at will, but is actually a perception albeit an incorrect one. In other words, we see, hear, smell, taste and feel things that aren't there. Hallucinations are fascinating to study but quite frightening to experience. For example, a person may think there are spiders crawling all over her body or may hear information about herself coming from a television that isn't on. Most hallucinations are auditory but I have had some that are visual, olfactory and tactile as well. They can be difficult to recognize in the acute stages of a mental illness like bipolar disorder because they can at times be mixed with realistic perceptions. During mania, I was most frightened and most aware of the hallucinations that were visual – these were the ones that made me feel like I was crazy.

There is much variability in the way that hallucinations are experienced by patients. Some are brief and infrequent while others may be quiet regular or lengthy. Except for one extended experience when I was in the hospital pharmacy, most of my hallucinations lasted between five and thirty seconds and some were clumped together.

Hallucinations may be experienced in a variety of locations as well. I experienced the first ones in my home, then some in the community and quite a few in the hospital before my treatment began. Some were more intense than others and had different effects on me. I was frightened and propelled into action by some of the visual ones and only slightly bothered by others.

In bipolar disorder, hallucinations usually occur in the most severely ill patients. Not everyone with the illness will experience them. They may be present with or without delusions but are among the least common symptoms experienced by patients. According to Redfield-Jamison (1990), hallucinations can often become one of the first symptoms to disappear once medical treatment is started. Fortunately, for me, this was true and I was profoundly relieved to be rid of them. It is interesting that a number of my hallucinations had a religious theme, which was fairly often reported by other patients I knew as well.

Hallucinations may indicate the beginning of psychosis and should serve as a serious red flag. Patients should ask for help immediately if experiencing them. Brain chemistry can be so unbalanced at this point that one may have little sense of self left.

My symptoms of bipolar disorder escalated and included hallucinations for about two weeks before my last hospital stay. The first were auditory and occurred mostly at night. I kept hearing a knocking at my apartment door and thought that someone was trying to break in. When I went to look, no-one was there but I was so convinced of an intruder that I called the police several times in the middle of the night. When they came to investigate, they of course found no-one in the building. However, I, in my paranoia, fetched a large carving knife from my kitchen and kept it under my bed. At this time, I didn't know I was hallucinating. The situation seemed very real to me and this particular hallucination continued right up to the time I was last hospitalized.

Other auditory hallucinations I can recall included the noise of children laughing outside in the middle of the night, the pervasive cry of a hawk outside my window, drawers slamming shut in my apartment, a crashing noise and the sound of a chair being dragged across a solid floor above me. (The apartments all have wall to wall carpeting). Sometimes, I also heard voices but I couldn't tell if they were inside my head or from the external environment. Some voices were comforting while others were quite threatening. I did find that the auditory hallucinations had less power over me if I was able to talk about them with someone.

My visual hallucinations were another story – a terrifying one. They came later, closer to the time I was admitted into the hospital. At that time, in my manic episode, I had lost several consecutive nights of sleep during my week-long attempt at getting admitted into psychiatric care. It was a bleak Thursday afternoon in November and after an initial assessment from the psychiatric crisis team, I was about to be sent home for the fourth time in the same week. I was handed another prescription for a drug that didn't work and was told to fill it in the hospital pharmacy. That's when I had the hallucination of the strange man who called me the "brown-eyed girl". I was bombarded by various other hallucinations of people during that day and was most distraught.

Over the next couple of days the hallucinations continued to worsen. Eventually, I didn't know who was real and who wasn't, from ambulance attendants, police officers, doctors and nurses to people I saw on the street. Everyone I looked at seemed to me to be talking about me and my illness, so I started to keep my head down when there were people around. If I looked up, it would only confirm that I was being chastised by others, or so I thought.

My most frightening hallucinations happened on the night prior to my hospitalization in November, 2006. I was at home, but completely psychotic; unable to discern what was real and what wasn't. I had been awake for two nights at this point. I turned on the television to block out the noises and voices I'd been hearing for some time. It was then that I saw demonic images on the screen. In addition, voices were telling me to give money to the devil and there was no escape. I had one hallucination after another. The experience was a combination of cognitive and emotional bedlam.

Hallucinations happen as a byproduct of neurobiological changes in the brain in bipolar disorder. They can be stopped by using appropriate antipsychotic medication and effects can be minimized by using strategies such as humming, singing, playing music, talking to others or reading aloud. A reduction in highly emotional triggers can also reduce the frequency and intensity of hallucinations.

Since they are such a striking component of bipolar disorder, I still have many questions about them. Why and exactly how do they happen? How is the brain involved and what part is involved? Why do there seem to be recurrent themes present, like that of religion? Hopefully, continued research will improve our knowledge of this troublesome symptom of bipolar disorder.

Delusions

To this date I don't recall all of the delusions I went through but I certainly had them. Many were identified by clinicians, friends and family members. Two in particular come to mind. Prior to my last hospitalization, I thought that I was a great orator and was going to conduct a lecture on psychosis for the entire medical staff of the hospital. That delusion was fleeting but I had another one that lasted for several days when I was a new patient in the psychiatric ward. I believed that I was a messenger from God that was sent to Earth in order to round up people to save the world. I also thought I was responsible for saving my roommate from evil and making her well even though I knew she was schizophrenic. Consequently, I told all the psychiatric patients on the ward what their role in saving the world was and that when they left the hospital, they must study whatever discipline was required of them in order to fulfill their roles. I must have sounded quite convincing (and grandiose) since on numerous occasions, patients would come to me with a plan of what they were going to do. Needless to say, the nurses quickly caught on and asked me not to discuss these matters with the patients and to mind my own business. Interestingly, they didn't argue with me but rather observed and advised which I suppose was less threatening.

Eventually, after a few days of medical intervention and treatment, I was talked out of my delusional state but I wasn't able to talk other patients out of theirs although I tried. Likely, this was a delicate process which only professionals would be trained to do.

Like my hallucinations, it was common for my delusions to have a religious theme. Yet, I certainly was not the only messenger of God on the ward. Feelings of religious inspiration were very common. It was interesting that when others professed their delusions to me, I was able to point out that they weren't accurate and yet I was convinced that I was God's true messenger. I had all sorts of stories to tell pertaining to this delusion. For example, I told others that I had been dead for a few minutes and had passed through God's judgement. I declared that God had a sense of humour and had put up an enormous neon "H" outside my window which stood for heaven! I advised the other patients that they had also been chosen to pass through judgement and that they must be good and noble so that they could go back into the world and fulfill their true mission before they really died for good!

When I experienced these delusions of supernatural knowledge, I felt as if every event had special significance and was related to God's plan for me. Thus, anyone who knew I was God's messenger would wink at me and that was an indication that others were also well informed about my mission.

Eventually, as the course of my treatment progressed, my delusions gradually faded away. I have never suffered delusions while depressed and only reached psychosis in mania. My delusions had made me think that trivial events were signs of tremendous significance and I had experienced an indescribable feeling of mental power while in a delusional state. Only after my medication began to work did I realize that my delusions were false beliefs which were causing all sorts of problems. After they subsided, I was embarrassed but relieved and I apologized to the patients I had misled.

Delusions are misconceptions about who we are and often what our purpose is. They are inaccurate but profound beliefs that can't be corrected by discussion or logic. Delusional individuals are alone in their perception and have either an exaggerated sense of self-worth when manic or utter worthlessness when depressed. Mania may be accompanied by the delusion that a person is responsible for saving the world while depression may bring on the feeling of being at fault for all of the world's problems. Manic patients experiencing delusions of grandeur may feel that they are special or have unique powers. For example, an individual might think he is a messenger from God, or Jesus himself or the devil. People who are depressed and delusional may hold inappropriate guilt or delusions of persecution – the belief that others are interfering in their lives. If patients become paranoid, they may have delusions that everyone (including people on the radio or television) is talking negatively about them, and they can't be convinced otherwise.

Some common delusions are as follows:

1. Delusions of grandeur – beliefs that a person is actually a great figure such as God or the devil. Often the holder believes that she has special powers.
2. Delusions of persecution – beliefs that a person is being interfered with by others. The patient often believes that he or she is being plotted against or followed. For example, an individual may think that the secret service has planted a camera in the ceiling of his or her room.
3. A somatic delusion is the false belief that something is wrong with one's body. In my case, I thought I had cancer at one point in my illness and telephoned many people to tell them so.
4. Delusions of control – beliefs that another person or outside force is controlling one's thoughts, feelings or actions, for example through a curse. In hospital, I placed a curse on a man at the dinner table one night.
5. Religious delusions – beliefs that a patient has religious importance such as being a biblical figure or messenger from God.

6. Paranoid delusions – beliefs that a person is in danger or the victim of evil people or forces.

Delusional thinking often disturbs others and gets a person into trouble. For example, an employee might give up her job to start an amazing new business without funding or credentials. It is important to understand however that delusions are not just ideas or passing thoughts; they are entrenched beliefs. They can also get worse as a psychotic episode progresses.

In summary, psychosis, including hallucinations and delusions, is an unwelcome foe and demands the utmost care in treating the patient. Medical intervention can eliminate these troubling symptoms and can help patients function better throughout their treatment regime.

Medication Non-Compliance

The reluctance of patients to take their medication is a major problem in bipolar disorder. Some studies suggest that fifty percent of patients discontinue their medication for a variety of reasons (Torry, Knable, 2005). This can result in serious relapses, further hospitalization, psychotic behaviour, spending sprees, homelessness and possible violence and jail time.

Some patients refuse their medication because they are not aware of their illness. The parts of the brain responsible for reflective thinking are not working properly and individuals don't believe they are ill. When I was initially diagnosed, I was one of these individuals. I refused to accept that I had bipolar disorder and took myself off medication several times. Because I didn't understand how bipolar disorder was manifested and due to troubling side effects ranging from mild depression and upset stomach to hair loss, I did not comply with physicians' instructions to stay on medication. At the time, I was diagnosed with bipolar II disorder and hadn't yet experienced a full manic episode. I was agitated, angry and defiant according to others but refused to think that there was anything wrong with me. I understood what depression was but didn't comprehend the symptoms of hypomania and thought that others were over-reacting to my behaviour. Even after I was hospitalized for the first time, I refused to acknowledge the illness or take the time to find suitable treatment. As a result, I struggled through yet another six months of bipolar disorder and nearly lost everything – my home, friends, family and my job.

I am now a very co-operative patient but had even more reasons to ignore the doctor's orders initially. Many patients complain of similar behaviour patterns prior to the acceptance of medical treatment. Some hypomanic or manic patients say they feel well and are troubled by the idea that medicine controls their moods. Patients have sometimes reported that they feel flat and that they miss the positives of hypomania. Side effects such as cognitive dulling, decreased energy or decreased enthusiasm may bother patients like me significantly. Some people report feeling less creative and less attractive to friends or partners. They are bothered by a diagnosis of a chronic illness.

Patients who turn away from medical treatment may not have been educated about the illness and thus have limited knowledge or insight about their condition. This is exactly what happened to me when I was first diagnosed as an out-patient. In addition, other problems that may have an effect on medication adherence include substance abuse, personality disorders or other co-morbid conditions. Some patients are bothered by the amount of time it takes for medication to work – several days for an anti-manic to possibly several weeks for an antidepressant.

Fortunately, it is my nature to research any diagnosis that has been attributed to me, and by the time I was treated in November, 2006, I knew what to expect and was therefore more compliant with physicians than I had been prior to that time.

In the long run, it is important for patients to find a caring doctor who they can trust to guide them through the difficult stages of the illness and through an effective treatment process. Emphatically, I must state that it is absolutely vital for patients who are medicated for bipolar disorder to follow their doctor's advice and stick to medications that work. The consequences of non-adherence can be distastrous.

Substance Abuse

Drug and alcohol abuse can create giant problems for people with bipolar disorder. Fortunately, I have never suffered the debilitating effects of substance abuse, but my father did, even though he wasn't officially diagnosed with bipolar disorder. However, in an attempt to self-medicate, he began abusing alcohol when I was ten or eleven, a time when his moods were very volatile. There were problems with his law practice and verbally violent confrontations with my mother as well. It was frightening enough to witness my dad's violent mood swings, but when he drank, things got even worse. At first, he would withdraw and brood over his problems, but if my mother was present, both my parents would let loose and I was too scared to leave them alone because both of them could be unpredictable and either of them could have been hurt. Stuck in the middle of altercations like theirs was no place for a child to be but I did not trust my parents, so for the next eight years I became involved in most of these battles.

By the time I was ten, I knew that people with problems could seek counselling, but neither of my parents were willing or able to reach out for support. My dad was therefore not officially diagnosed with bipolar disorder and either made up excuses for his drinking or blamed it on my mother or on problems with work. It is difficult for me to remember what came first – mood swings, drinking or marital troubles, but as the years progressed, the problems only got worse. I developed chronic anxiety, especially at night when most conflicts would erupt. I'll never forget the night of my high-school graduation, when I returned home with a few friends later on after the dance only to find my father in a drunken rage, threatening to poke my mother's eyes out. In retrospect, I should have called the police but I was probably desensitized to the effects that alcohol abuse had on my family and therefore didn't act. I have a vague memory of the next few days being very traumatic and including the threat that my dad would be leaving my mother for good. It took him a year to follow through with that commitment, but even after he left, he continued to drink (although the effects were less visible to me). Nevertheless, he continued to use alcohol to self medicate his unstable moods. Sadly, although he was eventually treated for depression, he never got the help he really needed for his mood disorder before he died.

My dear friend Michael, who also has bipolar disorder is a work in progress where alcohol and drug abuse are concerned. At age seventeen, he received his first diagnosis of depression and experimented with alcohol at that time, however, a diagnosis of bipolar disorder didn't come for several years. As a teenager, Michael loved hockey and became a highly skilled player. At nineteen, he suffered a broken back and discovered that he would never completely recover from this injury. Excruciating physical pain coupled with the emotional trauma of losing the sport he loved combined with emerging bipolar symptoms to bring about the abuse of alcohol at that time. As mental illness took hold of him, his substance abuse escalated to include cocaine and other drugs. He was devastated by the loss of hockey and continued to self-medicate with drugs and alcohol to numb both physical and mental pain. Then the addictions spiralled out of control and in 2005 he had his first breakdown. Michael has been in treatment for several years but recovery has been difficult. Nevertheless, he never gives up hope and is well aware of how substance abuse affects him and his loved ones. He is on the path to recovery.

With easy access to substances in the community, it is easy to see why substance abuse is so rampant in those with bipolar disorder. In addition, drug dealers know how to prey on this vulnerable population. Some studies estimate that approximately sixty percent of bipolar patients will at some point during their lives be dependent on drugs or alcohol (Torrey, Knable, 2005).

The reasons why bipolar disorder and substance addictions co-exist are not established but there are some theories. For example, there may be a shared predisposition to both substance abuse and bipolar disorder or there may be shared neurochemistry in both. A third hypothesis is that chronic substance abuse may cause bipolar disorder in some although there is no research to suggest a causal relationship. Another theory is that mania and hypomania influence the pursuit of enjoyable and high risk behaviour such as drinking and drug abuse. Fifthly, patients with addiction problems may be self medicating, attempting to eliminate symptoms of their illness. Finally, since substance addiction and bipolar disorder are fairly common, there may be a connection simply by chance.

Whatever the cause, substance addiction is highly destructive. Firstly, addictions may mask the diagnosis of bipolar disorder and individuals may be labelled as addicts before anyone realizes that they have a mental illness. Studies also indicate that bipolar patients who abuse substances suffer more disturbed mania, rapid cycling of episodes, mixed episodes, poorer response to medication, slower recovery rates, more relapses and hospitalizations, poorer job success and higher rates of suicide (Torrey, Knable, 2005).

The treatment of addictions is difficult enough without compounding bipolar disorder on top of it. Some medications may be less effective and delay recovery as a result. In addition, addicted people may be unwilling or unable to stop using substances until they have to deal with visible consequences such as violent crimes for example. Organizations such as Alcoholics Anonymous are helpful but concurrent substance addiction and bipolar disorder will continue to be a critical problem in the recovery from this illness.

Suicide

Bipolar disorder in its most severe form can be lethal. Suicide is a very real threat to bipolar patients and everything must be done to prevent its occurrence. This is not easy because often, suicidal patients don't tell their doctors the full extent of their ideas and plans. This lack of communication makes it difficult for clinicians to assess risk.

Currently, approximately twenty-five percent of bipolar individuals attempt suicide and somewhere between seven and ten percent actually achieve it (Redfield- Jamison, 2007, p. 956). Fortunately, during both depressive and manic phases of my illness, I did not feel suicidal even though I sometimes felt like I was dying. I never really wanted to kill myself. Others are not so lucky.

There are numerous risk factors that can serve as warnings for suicide and patients demonstrating any of these should be watched closely. Some critical risks include: having had a recent episode of mania, depression or mixed state, severe anxiety or panic attacks, severe sleep problems, recent losses (money, job, relationship), a family history of suicide, an aggressive, impulsive or risk-taking personality, concurrent substance abuse (especially alcohol), social isolation, poor response to medication and seasonal changes with spring being the most risky (Torrey, Knable, 2005). Other chronic risk factors include past suicide attempts, an absence of future orientation, severe physical illness, a history of violence or having weapons in the home (Redfield Jamison, 2007, p. 956).

In order to correctly assess suicide risk, patients must be asked specific questions about their thoughts, feelings and actions. While in the hospital emergency ward during my manic episode, I was assessed for suicide risk because I apparently (although I don't remember it) conveyed to an intake psychiatrist that I would slit my wrist if I was not admitted to the hospital. As a result, even though I was saying that out of desperation, I spent the first night in isolation and observation, was reassessed the next day and found to be risk free. Nevertheless, I was asked about my feelings and thoughts about death, about previous attempts to harm myself (there were none), if I had a suicide plan, if others in my family had been suicidal and if I felt that life was over for me. I was also asked if I heard voices telling me to harm myself (I heard voices but no commands) and whether I wanted to harm or kill anyone else.

Even though I was not identified as suicidal, a number of protective measures were put in place in order to keep me safe. Firstly, I was placed in a locked psychiatric unit. Secondly, I was initially situated in an observation and crisis room and was not allowed any of my personal possessions for the first night. Also, for the first two days, I had to have a nurse stand outside the washroom with the door ajar while I showered. I had to use plastic cutlery after admission and was not allowed access to any sharp objects. These restrictions remained in place until I was medicated for the illness.

There are a number of personal attributes that help protect bipolar patients from suicide. Some of these include overall life satisfaction, coping skills, having a family to look after, a strong, supportive social network, good interpersonal skills, resourcefulness, motivation to get help, religious involvement, intelligence, creativity, problem-solving skills, overall good health and a willingness to follow a prescribed treatment plan. I feel fortunate to have a good number of these attributes and I cannot emphasize enough the need to follow one's prescribed treatment plan. As a result, I can confidently predict that I will remain well enough that I will not ever be at risk for suicide. My doctors carefully balanced my need for independence with safety factors and I am now back on my feet.

However, despite everyone's best efforts, some bipolar patients will commit suicide, but loved ones should not feel guilty or blame themselves. Without a doubt, suicide in bipolar individuals is tragic and has a devastating and lifelong effect on those left behind.

CHAPTER 6
THE TREATMENT OF
BIPOLAR DISORDER

The treatment of bipolar disorder remained difficult until the middle of the twentieth century when lithium was discovered. This drug saved many lives and is still widely used today. Currently , bipolar disorder is treated with medication and a variety of forms of psychotherapy.

For over twenty years I have known that I needed help, but what was always puzzling was that I didn't know why. In the late fall and early spring of nearly every year, I would experience depressions serious enough to warrant therapy and medication. Then there were times when I felt highly agitated or out of control and during those times, I would spend money like crazy without knowing that this behaviour was a symptom of bipolar disorder. In addition, I couln't understand why I experienced such high degrees of anxiety and agitation, but thought these symptoms were related to Tourette's

Syndrome which was diagnosed when I was in my early thirties. I was treated for that condition with therapy and medication for thirteen years, until the symptoms of Tourette's went into remission. Then, almost at the drop of a hat, I was diagnosed with bipolar II disorder. It was all very confusing and honestly, I really didn't know what I had.

I was introduced to treatment with medication only at first. The diagnosis of bipolar II disorder was suggested rather than confirmed and at the time, I was not cognizant of the ways in which the illness was manifested, or how it affected me and others around me. It was a baffling time. Firstly, lithium was prescribed (a common mood stabilizer) and I began to take it at about the same time as I started to research the illness. Within days, I experienced severe stomach pains and headaches. Hoping that the side effects would abate, I stuck with it for several months. Lithium works well for many people but within a couple of weeks, I felt that I had lost all of my energy, creativity, sense of humour and indeed my whole personality. I felt flat, and even mildly depressed, but definitely not myself. My mother told me that I was just like everyone else, and at that point, I thought that it must be better to be ill rather than exist in a drug induced fog. Nevertheless, I continued taking lithium for three months. Had I received psychotherapy at that time along with the medication, I might have fared better.

When the side effects of lithium still persisted, I asked my doctor to take me off it. Shortly afterwards, I went to see a neurologist as I was having great difficulty with short-term memory and disorientation. I couldn't remember anything and was highly absent-minded. The neurologist agreed with the previous psychiatrist's diagnosis and placed me on an anti-convulsant (which can also be used as a mood stabilizer) called valproaic acid. Again, this medication works well for some people, but didn't for me. Still, without therapy, I was not convinced that I had bipolar disorder. I was persistant in emphasizing to others that there was nothing wrong with me except for occasional short bouts of mild depression which usually passed given time. So, after a couple of months, valproate was discontinued and I convinced my family physician (but not my psychiatrist) that I was fine.

However, shortly thereafter, even I began noticing erratic behaviour in myself. By this time, I was likely a little more self-aware having done some research on bipolar disorder. At any rate, I became very agitated and decided suddenly that I had to move to a new home! In addition, I either drove like a maniac or periodically fell asleep at the wheel after nights of insomnia. I couldn't sleep at night or wake up properly in the morning. I missed so much work that I had to go on a medical leave of absence. Then, while in the process of moving, I decided to sell my car and do without. In the process of cancelling my lease, I aggravated and ruined relationships with a number of people and I was highly unstable. I was not on any medication at this time and was having outbursts of rage while at the same time dealing with these other issues. My mother tried to help me through this period, but I was beyond hope. I began to have panic attacks and tearful outbursts and would make up stories to explain my behaviour to others. In a crisis, I finally did move (to my current address) and got rid of my car. This was October, 2005, six months prior to my first hospitalization. While all this was going on, I created a huge rift between my mother and me and I did not spend Christmas with my family that year.

My friends and family pleaded with me to go back on lithium since it made me, "more like us". However, I felt that all of them were dull, boring and unemotional and I didn't want to be like them. Yet, I also knew that I was not behaving normally and so agreed to try lithium again. Had I received psychotherapy at that point, as an intervention, I may have been able to stop the progression of the illness, but I didn't seek that kind of help at the time. As a result, I took myself off lithium once more within a few weeks of starting due to gastrointestinal side-effects and emotional flatness.

Somehow, I muddled through the rest of the winter without medication, but I was not well and I knew it. For some reason, I have very little memory of what happened over the next few months and have had to rely on others to report on my behaviour during that time. Rumour has it that I was overbearing, demanding, overly gregarious and rude.

Types of Treatment
Medication

Bipolar disorder is treated with a variety of medications which help to stabilize mood. For mania, the medications include: lithium, some antiepileptic drugs including valproate, antipsychotics such as chlorpromazine, haloperidol, perphenazine, thioridazine and atypical antipsychotics such as olanzapine, clozapine, risperidone, quetiapine, ziprazidone and aripiprazole (Suppes et all, 2007, p. 217).

It wasn't until I was admitted to the hospital for the second time that I became a co-operative patient and agreed to stay until effective medication could be tried and tested on me over time. After extensive interviews, observation and familiarization with my treatment history, It was decided that I would try olanzapine (Zyprexa), an atypical antipsychotic that can be used as a mood stabilizer as well. In addition, the antipsychotic properties of the medication served to reduce, then eventually eliminate my delusions and hallucinations.

After a few days, it appeared that we had hit the jackpot! My psychosis abated and I felt much better. I was starting to make sense when talking with others and was less disoriented. The mania subsided gradually and I was able to participate more effectively in the rest of the treatment program. Because I responded so well to Zyprexa, the dosage was gradually increased until I stabilized about a week later. I did gain weight, but accepted that it would be my job to do something about it and that I had been fortunate to find a medication that made me feel well again. I remained a little unsure of myself and a bit disorganized for a few weeks after my hospital stay, but I was delighted to be released from the hospital only ten days after admission. Originally, I had thought that I would need months of medical treatment before a successful outcome would be reached.

I presently take twenty milligrams of olanzapine (Zyprexa) as a mood stabilizer and 125 milligrams of clomipramine – an antidepressant used to treat anxiety. Many patients with bipolar disorder also have co-morbidities. Some patients and clinicians find that antidepressants have a tendency to increase mania but I have never experienced that outcome. I have chosen to remain on these medications despite the side effect of weight gain because the benefits far outweigh the costs. Believe me, it is much better to be sane than skinny!

Medical Treatment of Mania, Hypo-mania and Mixed States

For patients dealing with manic symptoms, education, persuasion to follow a treatment regimen and medication are key components of an overall treatment program. Individuals with severe or psychotic mania will likey require hospitalization, possibly involuntarily. Effective medication is key for highly agitated, manic patients. Antipsychotic medications are usually used for emergency treatment, then within the first few days, doctors will be able to discern whether the manic symptoms will abate slowly or quickly. When I was treated for mania during my last hospital stay, I had already experienced the effects of numerous medications. It was decided very quickly to try olanzapine and I was relatively stable within two weeks. Since my manic episode was psychotic and included hallucinations and delusions, an atypical antipsychotic was chosen as opposed to a common mood stabilizer or anticonvulsant.

Medical treatment of Depression in Bipolar Disorder

I have been depressed many times throughout the course of my life for short periods of time, and managed without medication until I was twenty-eight and experiencing the breakdown of my marriage. At that point in time, I also experienced anxiety and panic that was so debilitating that I was close to being suicidal and had to be medicated quickly in order to regain some self-control. There was no assessment of bipolar disorder at that time however, and I was without a doubt, devastated and couldn't function. My psychiatrist prescribed imipramine, a tricyclic antidepressant, and Xanax, an anti-panic medication. The dosages were increased more quickly than usual since I was unable to function and had just been hired as a teacher in the public school board. It took well over a month, however, for the medication to have some effect in reducing the panic but I continued to be depressed until I made the decision to leave my marriage and the matrimonial home. At that point, about three months later, I stopped taking Xanax, but remained on imipramine for another three months, until I was better adjusted to my new living situation which included a new home a new job and a new life! My psychiatrist then tapered the dosage gradually until I was free of medication altogether, but I relapsed a month later and had to go back on it. I didn't realize at that point that my depression had been somewhat reactive, but also clinical. Thus, a lower maintenance dosage was established and I was once again able to function.

Over the course of the next couple of years, I tried twice to withdraw from the imipramine but for some reason, I relapsed each time. By the time I turned thirty-one, I had been diagnosed with Tourette's Syndrome and was placed on a related tricyclic medication called clomipramine (supposedly to help with some mild obsessive compulsive disorder). I was also treated with haloperidol in order to decrease the tics associated with that disorder. My new psychiatrist advised me that I would remain on both medications over the long term.

Despite the medication, there were still times when I felt depressed and\or severely agitated over the years, especially in the spring and fall, and I was a poor sleeper. I felt that these depressions were triggered by external events and I would seek out counselling for short periods of time in order to resolve my issues. This pattern went on for nearly fifteen years until my Tourette's psychiatrist first diagnosed me with bipolar disorder and explained to me that I would need a mood stabilizer to complement the clomipramine.

Treatment of Depression in Bipolar Disorder

The diagnosis of depression in bipolar disorder can be difficult because clinicians must determine if the patient is suffering from unipolar depression or the bipolar form of the illness. Also, the depressed person's response to medication is slower than a manic person's response. Bipolar depression can be dangerous as most bipolar suicides occur when patients are in this state.

When medicated, patients gain back their energy before their mood improves. As a result, individuals who have been so severely depressed that they have been unable to act on their feelings become more likely to attempt suicide. It is therefore important to hospitalize severely depressed patients so that the effects and side effects of medication can be observed closely. It may take several weeks before the benefits of medication can be observed, and several months before full improvement can be seen.

Many depressed bipolar patients improve with lithium alone but there are often comorbid conditions such as anxiety or insomnia (I have both) which require the addition of other medications such as benzodiazepines or antidepressants. Care must be given in administering antidepressants as patients may experience an acute manic switch. Fortunately, this did not happen to me and I continue to take antidepressant medication along with olanzapine. Some of the more recent antidepressants, the SSRI's are less likely than older tricyclic antidepressants to cause a manic switch.

If bipolar patients are dealing with substance abuse, treatment is complicated and may take months or even years to be totally effective. I met a number of patients in the hospital who had been in for months and one for over a year because they needed to detox from drugs and alcohol as part of their treatment. A significant number of patients with bipolar disorder suffer from addictions and may need longer treatment programs.

The Side Effects of Medication

Some patients on lithium suffer gastrointestinal difficulties as a side effect. There have also been complaints about poor concentration, poor memory and fine tremors. Unfortunately, I did experience these symptoms during two separate trials of lithium. This medication works very well for many people but it was not the right medication for me. Recent research on olanzapine has indicated that weight gain, especially abdominally can be expected with this medication. There is also an increased risk of diabetes. Therefore, patients must be counselled about the need for a healthy diet and regular exercise. Olanzapine is a medication which has worked extremely well for me as a mood stabilizer and antipsychotic. It has enabled me to feel quite normal. However, I do struggle with the additional weight gain that is associated with this medication and I must maintain a healthy regimen of diet and vigorous activity. Happily, I have not been diagnosed with diabetes. Despite the weight gain, I do not suffer any other identifiable side effects at present. When olanzapine was first administered to me in the hospital, I had some unusual short-term side effects such as headaches and night sweats, however, these subsided within a week. Presently, I have good concentration, an improved memory and a stable sense of self. I do not feel that my personality has been altered by olanzapine, but I do notice some loss of creative ability. The important thing to realize about side effects is that everyone is different in their response to medication and sometimes, It takes time to find the most suitable medical treatment.

Psychotherapy

Any part of a comprehensive treatment program for patients with bipolar disorder includes psychotherapy as well as medication. In my case, psychotherapy took several forms and was administered by a number of professionals. During my first hospital stay, when I was clearly in denial about my illness, I did not respond favourably to medication or therapy. When I was hospitalized again six months later, I knew I needed help and was much more open to therapy. I was psychotic and frightened and knew that I needed care. I resolved to listen to and follow all the advice and counselling from the professionals involved in my case.

First of all, I was assigned to a compassionate psychiatrist who took a great deal of time with me in confirming the diagnosis of bipolar I disorder. As part of the evaluation, she interviewed me in depth, took a family history and observed me closely. She asked me about my symptoms and asked further questions about my safety and my support network. She also questioned me about stressors in my life and briefed me about the nature of the treatment I would receive at the hospital. We discussed the effects of various medications I had tried and then, almost by default, decided on olanzapine. This psychiatrist met with me daily after breakfast to see how I was doing and to discuss issues. Luckily, she was my case co-ordinator as well as my psychiatrist and she orchestrated therapy through all of the other professionals involved.

As an inpatient, I was also assigned to a general practitioner who came to see me every morning before breakfast. He inquired about my physical well-being and made dietary and exercise recommendations. He emphasized that I would likely have to change my lifestyle in order to combat the side effects of olanzapine such as weight gain.

The team of psychiatric nurses on the unit were invaluable to me. They observed me closely and interacted with me enough to ensure that I was comfortable. In addition, they conducted support groups in stress management, psychology, fitness, recreation and symptom management. They helped me to structure my days and went beyond the call of duty to get to know me better. The nurses also helped set up other services I would need as an inpatient and later as an outpatient. For example, when I attempted shoplifting while in a psychotic state, I found out that I would have to go through what is called a mental health diversion court process to get the charges dropped. I would need to speak with a court support worker in order to get that process going. I did, later after my release, have to appear in court on four separate dates over the course of one year, but the charges were dropped due to the fact that I had a mental illness.

During my inpatient stay, my therapist arranged for a psychiatric nurse to come to my home once per month once I was released. That particular nurse was extremely resourceful and valuable to me. She was instrumental in helping me develop, follow and ultimately succeed in a debt repayment program from a credit counselling service. My therapist also set up monthly meetings with an outpatient psychiatrist that I see to this day.

In order for psychotherapy to be effective for bipolar patients, there are a number of elements which should be in place. First of all, the therapist needs to conduct a thorough diagnostic evaluation which includes interviews, observations and a family psychiatric history. The patient's safety should be determined and a course of treatment must be established. A therapeutic relationship must be developed between doctor and patient and the therapist must monitor the patient's response to treatment. It is extremely important to educate the patient about bipolar disorder including what to expect, current trends and available resources. The therapist must do everything possible to enhance the patient's adherence to medication and to minimize side effects. In addition, the patient's awareness of stressors and patterns of sleep and activity must be made clear and the therapist needs to educate the patient regarding early signs of relapse. It is also necessary to determine difficulties in functioning in the patient's life. For example, I still have much difficulty sleeping and I experience some cognitive impairment regarding creative ideation and memory. However, I was educated by my therapist about the personal, interpersonal and social repercussions of bipolar disorder which can be serious and can include suicide, violence, divorce, alchoholism, drug abuse, hospitalization and unemployment. Patients should be told that the nature of their illness includes psychological and behavioural indicators. Psychotherapy can also help to alter the progression of the natural path of the illness. It certainly did with me.

It is essential for therapists not to attempt to control the patient too much and not to become involved in a power struggle with her. Therapists must artfully balance the patient's need for independence with his or her need for intervention. For example, the patient may need help to deal with a variety of issues such as career change, finances, alienation from others, medical expenses, legal problems, poor self-confidence and addictions. I was informed about a drug benefit plan for people with disabilities called "Trillium", and also was advised about mental health court diversion and about credit counselling services. These were all very necessary supports for me (even though my ultimate success depended on my own actions), because I was far too overwhelmed to put these things in place myself or even to know what I needed during the crisis phase of my illness.

My entire treatment team consisted of an inpatient and outpatient psychiatrist, an inpatient and outpatient general practitioner, a social worker, a court support officer, inpatient and outpatient psychiatric nurses, a recreation director and a peer group facilitator.

When I look back and reflect on my last stay at the hospital, I realize that I couldn't have asked for more. Things ran like clockwork and it was fairly easy for me to make the transition from inpatient therapy to an outpatient day treatment program once I was released. I had originally thought that it would take six to eight weeks for the clinicians to figure me out, but I was comfortably ready to go home in less than two weeks. After my release, I immediately began day treatment – a daily six hour program which was three weeks in duration. Thanks to the group facilitators and feedback from other patients, I learned some valuable lessons in day treatment. Instruction regarding medication adherence, making good judgments, handling financial difficulties and dealing with interpersonal conflict was provided. I was taught to see bipolar disorder as a medical illness and to communicate to others without the stigma often attached to mental illness. Clinicians taught me what to expect – some ups and downs, residual disorientation until I was fully adjusted to medication and the experience of loss I might feel because of the illness or the medication. In addition, I was instructed to use a day-book or journal to monitor my moods and to help me structure my days.

Some patients received career counselling or vocational rehabilitation in the day treatment program. During this time, I completed a thorough workbook on bipolar disorder which instructed me on such issues as power of attorney, making a list of contacts, documenting the effects of medications and listing warning signs that I might be in crisis or suffering a relapse. There is information beside my contact list that includes instructions on what legal professionals should do if I break the law or get arrested while I am sick. Fortunately, I know that if I adhere to my medication regimen and follow the rest of my treatment program carefully, I am not likely to commit any further offenses.

The therapeutic approach used in day treatment was called cognitive-behavioural therapy or CBT – a method of using thoughts to manage behaviour and emotions. For example, we were taught to use anti-manic cognitive techniques consisting of the early identification of thoughts, restructuring of these thoughts and evaluation of plans before taking action.

In order to treat patients effectively, there are a variety of attributes that clinicians and counsellors should have including: the ability to be respectful, to be compassionate and non-judgemental, and to be considerate, confidential, resourceful and experienced in dealing with bipolar disorder. Counsellors should be interested in their patients and should be professional at all times.

When dealing with therapists, patients must remember that their doctors do not have magical powers or all the answers, but are part of the overall treatment team. A large part of the recovery process involves not only medication and therapy, but ultimately, responsible action and open communication from the patient herself.

The combination of medical and therapeutic treatment for bipolar disorder should offer hope for the millions of patients who suffer and for their families and caregivers. Perhaps the most salient feature of a comprehensive treatment program is education. Ultimately, patients want to be in control of their own destiny and therefore, have a responsibility to learn as much as they can about the disorder and the methods used to treat it. Patients are encouraged to use the references listed at the back of this book as well as the many articles and on-line references available.

CHAPTER 7
OTHER ISSUES

The Trouble with Sleep

Sleep eludes me. Ever since I was a young child (age seven or so), I have had difficulty getting to sleep. Primarily, I have suffered from pervasive insomnia for most of my life. For many years, I coped poorly with this, often getting anxious about how many hours of sleep I was losing and fretting as the clock ticked away through the early hours of the morning. Somehow, I made it through elementary and highschool, although I often dozed off in class and was regularly late for school since I couldn't get up in the morning. I was not allowed to take any sleep medication as a youngster even though the problem was chronic. Doctors didn't know what to do with me, nor did my teachers who would often have to give me more than one prompt to answer a question or participate in a class discussion.

As I got older, the nature of my sleep disturbance began to change. I started to experience bursts of energy well into the evening and found nights better for doing homework or studying. I began to use the night productively rather than to lie in bed watching the clock. As a result, I soon experienced even more difficulty getting up in the morning and this pattern has worsened over time. It is still a problem to this day.

By the time I was in university, the stress caused by the sheer volume and complexity of the work I was doing contributed to my sleep disorder. I began to experience entire nights, sometimes two in a row when I could not get to sleep at all. After these sleepless nights, I would often have panic attacks and would be unable to function. The state of affairs perpetuated a vicious cycle of insomnia, difficulty waking and poor coping. I knew a little about proper sleep hygiene (for example, going to bed at the same time each night and getting up at the same time every morning), but try as I might, I was unable to adhere to such a routine because of chronic insomnia. Even if I was exhausted, I couldn't sleep. What I didn't know at the time was that I was also suffering from a circadian rhythm disorder which has to do with sleeping in the dark and waking in the light. Often, bipolar patients suffer from this. My circadian rhythm became completely reversed by the time I was twenty and remains so even today. I survived university by working late into the night, sleeping in the next day and juggling courses so that most of them were scheduled in the late afternoon or evening. In those days, this strategy helped to a degree as I was living in residence and my schedule didn't bother anyone else. I completed university with honours and then, with sleep disturbance in tow, faced the world of full time employment.

Hired as a social worker in a group home for delinquent girls, on the evening shift from five p.m. to one a.m., I managed to survive. However, the position, counselling these young federal offenders was highly stressful and I began to experience sleepless nights again. For one year, I stayed on at the home as a social worker, then decided to teach and enrolled at the University of Toronto for a degree in education. Chronic insomnia and difficulty waking created significant distress and I was either perpetually late for class or absent all together due to sleep deprivation. I was somehow able to complete my assignments on time but could not adjust to the daily routine. Again, I graduated with honours – luckily, but what was I thinking, undertaking a career where punctuality was paramount.

In my first teaching position which was at a private school, I was repeatedly late for work and spent most mornings in a fog, exhausted, and I would often not come around until one or two in the afternoon. I felt awful most of the time, and had blurred vision and memory problems due to sleep deprivation. On several occasions, I nearly lost my job because I was late or just couldn't function in the morning. The matter was very serious. I began to take over-the-counter sleep medication to help with the insomnia but it had no effect or at best worked for only a few days. I just could not get myself to feel drowsy at normal hours in the evening. Even the daily routine of teaching did not seem to correct my circadian rhythm difficulties.

Eventually, I pulled myself together enough to be on time for work (temporarily) but I still felt terrible in the mornings.

Then in 1988 my marriage of four years fell apart and I plunged into my first episode of clinical depression. In addition to insomnia, I suffered early morning waking at three or four a.m. every day for several months. My vision became impaired and I suffered through debilitating panic attacks (no doubt made worse because of sleep impoverishment). At that time, I was prescribed medication for sleep but it would only work for one or two nights before insomnia set in again.

Finally, when I realized that I would have to leave my marriage and move out on my own, the early morning waking and acute depression subsided. However, it should come as no surprise that the chronic insomnia persisted and actually started to get worse. Initially, I was hypervigilant when living alone and could not relax at night. Gradually, over the years, I adjusted to my new living arrangement and no longer felt anxious about losing sleep. If I couln't fall asleep, I would get up and read or plan lessons and mark work until five or six in the morning, then would doze off for an hour or two before going to work. It took every ounce of energy I had to make it to school on time, and safely.

For a number of years during my late twenties and early thirties, I was marginally able to cope with sleep loss and I could survive by catching up on the weekends. However, as I entered my forties, the insomnia again began to worsen and I started to miss work because I was simply unable to function. At the time, I was still being treated for Tourette's Syndrome and without a diagnosis of bipolar disorder, didn't realize that my problems with sleep could be related to the illness.

As I entered my mid-forties, I began to experience a greater number of bipolar symptoms and eventually had to terminate my employment as a teacher. Despite efforts by clinicians to treat my sleep disorder with medications, I still couldn't sleep and would quickly develop a tolerance for each new medication. I sometimes wonder whether my living situation helps or hinders me. I live alone, and therefore, don't have to adjust to a partner's routine, however, I was never really able to do that anyway, even when I was married.

Presently, I experience between one and three nights per week where I can't fall asleep at all. Then I have to catch up on hours missed and I sometimes oversleep as a result. I have tried nearly every sedative and sleep medication on the market but I either do not respond to these medications or else develop a tolerance for them within a few days. I have to be fairly possessive about sleep when I do get it since a significant loss of it can aggravate mania and I don't want to go through that again. At times, I am so exhausted during the day that I don't function well. I try to maintain good sleep habits, yet I have insomnia nearly every night so I sometimes have to get up at different times. Proper sleep is something that I am always working on yet my problems have been life-long and at this point, I don't expect them to fully abate although long periods of strenuous exercise do help. I will likely continue to experience bursts of energy at night as usual and regular bouts of insomnia.

Overall, sleep difficulties are a major component of bipolar disorder and can occur in several forms.

Circadian Rhythm Disorders

One of the most common symptoms of bipolar disorder is a reversed circadian rhythm (which means there is a tendency to be awake at night and asleep during the day). Most people however have an inner biological clock which helps to regulate the sleep-wake cycle. The brain's production of melatonin usually helps the body respond appropriately to darkness and light. In healthy individuals, melatonin is secreted at night promoting sleepiness, and is suppressed during the day causing wakefulness. In my case and in the case of many others with bipolar disorder, this system is reversed. Unfortunately, I failed to respond favourably to melatonin therapy and regressed quickly into a deep depression upon taking it, and therefore, treatment had to be stopped. For other patients, maintenance of consistent sleep-wake cycles is an essential therapeutic treatment.

Insomnia

On a good night, I can fall asleep in an hour or so. However, I rarely have a good night where sleep is concerned. Regardless of how tired I am during the day, my level of alertness increases after eight p.m. I have more energy at night and I am better able to focus then as well. In fact, most of this book was written between the hours of eight p.m. and five a.m.

I have insomnia, which is the inability to fall asleep. If I can't get to sleep in over an hour, I get up and read, work on this book or watch television until I get tired. I often don't get to sleep before daylight as a result, but in recent years, I have become quite impatient with myself when it comes to staying in bed for hours. I consider it a huge waste of time. Sometimes, within a few hours, I will get tired and go back to bed. Since I rarely feel drowsy, I have to rely on different cues to indicate to me that I am tired. For example, when I'm reading and notice my eyes wandering over the page or when my vision becomes blurry while watching television, I know that I'm tired. When morning arrives, I am either in a deep sleep or still awake from the night before. Either way, it often takes me until the afternoon to pull out of this sleepy state. This scenario has made it difficult for me to drive in the morning, and actually, when my bipolar disorder started to worsen a few years ago, I had a few harrowing moments when I fell asleep at the wheel. I am no longer as disoriented as I was at the pinnacle of my illness, but have chosen not to drive or have the expense of a car while I am paying off debt and starting to save.

Early Morning Waking and Oversleeping

Just over twenty years ago when I suffered my first and most profound depressive episode, I consistently woke up at three or four a.m. and was unable to get back to sleep. Because of chronic insomnia, I suffered at both ends of the sleep cycle. Many patients suffering from persistent early morning waking are also experiencing a depressive episode. These same people may have a tendency to oversleep. If I'm feeling a bit down, I also oversleep, and in fact, one problem tends to feed the other so I try not to do it regularly.

Sleep and Mood

The nature of a patient's environment can have a significant effect on his or her mood, and the nature of sleep is part of this. Therefore, it is crucial for bipolar patients to seek support in stabilizing sleep as much as possible in order to abet possible episodes of depression or mania. Rapid-cycling bipolar patients may be at increased risk due to an unregulated circadian rhythm. I am lucky to have found an effective mood stabilizing medication to control my mood since I am not able to maintain a 24 hour day-night cycle. At times, in fact, I operate more on a 48 hour cycle, but as my physical stamina continues to improve, I have found that lengthy, vigorous exercise help to a degree. Even though I am presently in a recovery phase of bipolar disorder, I have a more variable circadian rhythm than a person without bipolar disorder would have. It should be noted that several of my family members have also suffered from sleep disorders and it has in fact been demonstrated that circadian rhythm disorders could be inherited (Redfield -Jamison, Goodwin, 2007, p. 688). In any case, where sleep is concerned, I am an enigma; a work in progress and I will continue to explore treatments and strategies to improve the situation.

Bipolar Disorder in Children and Adolescents

At six years old, Matthew was already an accomplished little artist. He loved to paint, draw and sculpt, and would spend hours focussed on his artwork.

He could be polite, cheerful and endearing but he had another side to him – a dark side. One day, he came back to my classroom (I was his homeroom teacher) from a social studies integration and my child and youth worker asked him to remove his hat. Matthew immediately flew into a rage, screaming obscenities and hurling an ice skate at the youth worker's head. It didn't hit her thankfully, but she was rendered useless by this behaviour. Matthew was escorted by me to a time-out room where he continued to rage but was not in a position to hurt anyone else.

The only thing we could predict about Matthew was that he was unpredictable, and when he was agitated, his negative behaviour was severe. It would often take hours for him to come down from a rage attack and he frequently had to be escorted to our time-out room. Eventually, however, he would calm down, apologize tearfully and ask to come back to class. Then, often, he would function normally for days. At other times, Matthew would become overactive, giddy and loud and would disrupt the class with his antics.

This was Matthew twenty years ago. At that time, doctors and psychiatrists were stumped regarding his diagnosis. It wasn't until later in his teenage years that he finally got a diagnosis of bipolar disorder. Since throughout my career, I was a teacher for children with psychiatric and developmental disabilities, I observed a number of children wtih similar symptoms. A few of my more recent students did receive a correct diagnosis, but sadly, I never found out what happened to some of the other children since they moved on from my class.

There has been much more research in recent years about how bipolar disorder profiles in children and adolescents. Children's symptoms may differ substantially from those of adults but diagnostics have recently improved. Children with bipolar disorder are at increased risk for educational and serious behavioural difficulties and there may be a risk of suicide as well. These children often have much difficulty getting out of bed in the morning and are often late for school. Many also have problems with their internal temperature and are often too hot. I was very much like this as a child but didn't yet have the behavioural components of bipolar disorder. Other childhood symptoms include increased motor activity, increased crying, a high state of arousal, aggressiveness, impulsivity, grandiosity, difficulty separating from their mother, a craving for sweets and sleep disturbances (Papolos and Papolos, 2006, p. 174).

Redfield -Jamison and Goodwin (2007, p. 188) describe manic behaviour in children as an excessively happy or giddy mood, with increased goal orientation, heightened silliness, racing thoughts, daredevil behaviours, increased energy, hypersexuality, agitation, defiance, excessive sociability, teasing, problems on the bus, off-task behaviour and hallucinating. Other symptoms may include lying, rapid speech, paranoia and destruction of property.

On the other hand, bipolar children suffering from depression have a profound sense of hopelessness and may even become suicidal. Often comormid conditions exist such as attention deficit hyperactivity disorder (ADHD), obsessive-compulsive disorder (OCD), oppositional defiant disorder, conduct disorder, anxiety or even alcohol abuse (Redfield -Jamison and Goodwin, 2007 p. 190). These children are often in need of medication and hospitalization. In children, there is a greater prevalence of mixed states and rapid cycling when compared with adults.

There has recently been an increased awareness of mood disorders in teenagers and therefore, improvement in the diagnosis and treatment of bipolar disorder in this age group. Bipolar teens may be dealing with substance abuse, personality disorders, conduct disorders, grandiosity, risky behaviour, excessive spending or dangerous driving. Trends indicate that teenagers demonstrate more psychotic behaviours than adults do, are more likely to have mixed episodes, drop out of school, be male, never marry, be involved in minor crimes and have financial problems (Redfield-Jamison and Goodwin, 2007, p. 197).

Even with improvements, the correct diagnosis of bipolar disorder in children and youth can still be a problem. Many, diagnosed solely with ADHD or other disorders are actually going through the early stages of bipolar disorder. It is a problem that the DSM IV does not currently delineate criteria for children. There are no laboratory tests that can be used to diagnose bipolar disorder and diagnosis must be made from a combination of self-reportinig, family history, family interviews and observation. Also, in very young patients, it is hard to know how the illness will run its course and how it will impact their developmental histories. Finally, there are ethics regarding treatment and the administration of medication such as lithium or atypical antipsychotics, which may have profound side effects.

Fortunately, I did not have bipolar disorder as a child but did have some symptoms which may have overlapped with those of Tourette's Syndrome such as sleeplessness, a faulty internal thermometer, difficulty getting up in the morning and anxiety. Hopefully, ongoing improvements in the diagnosis and treatment of youngsters with bipolar disorder will continue so that these young patients will receive appropriate care and will suffer less as a result.

A Sense of Self

Who am I exactly? Where does my illness end and where do I begin? What is my true personality like? I ask myself these questions almost daily. I have been taking psychiatric medication for over twenty years, first after being diagnosed (albeit incorrectly) with unipolar depression, secondly, following a diagnosis of Tourette's Syndrome and thirdly for bipolar disorder. Presently, I feel quite "normal" and am described as such by the people around me. However, I often wonder if I have ever, in fact, been normal. I knew something was amiss as early as age six and have always thought of myself as different. Since I was initially a shy child, I knew that I would always have to work at fitting in socially – usually I was successful – sometimes not. Fortunately, during this recovery phase of my life, I now have supportive family members and friends but I realize that I didn't always feel this way. Looking back over the years, I notice that parts of my sense of self have changed while other components have remained constant. Generally, I now feel comfortable in my own skin, essentially, but I still wonder if there is a true self that I haven't discovered yet, a self that exists despite medication and the diagnosis of bipolar disorder. I suppose I am a whole person but perhaps there is more or less to me than the sum of the various parts.

If memory serves me correctly, I believe I was usually a good-natured and well-behaved child and had friends since my preschool years. I am still close to one of those friends, in fact. Although somewhat prone to nervousness and anxiety in my youth, I have always been self-aware (except perhaps when manic) and worked at getting past these negative feelings. At times, I would experience rages when very young, but they usually erupted as a reaction to highly troubling situations.

By middle childhood, as a result of being teased about my Tourette's tics, I realized that I was different. I knew that in order to be like everyone else, I was going to have to learn to hide my tics at school and around friends. By grade four, I was usually successful at this, except for eye blinking and found that I could release the tics at home in my room after school days were over. By age nine, I was able to finally finish my work on time without being distracted by my own movements and although I had always done fairly well in school, did even better and managed to skip grade four. However, little was known about Tourette's Syndrome in those days so no diagnosis was forthcoming at that time.

By the time I was eleven, my pervasive shyness really began to haunt me and I often wished that I was someone else or that I could change my personality. I became very aware that this trait was not serving me well and wanted to do something about it. My mother encouraged me to smile more (she still does) and I consciously put in an effort to do this, especially since I'd reached the age when I started to notice boys. I think it helped that I was part of a group of friends that I stayed with until the end of public school. It was fortunate that I skipped grade four since many of my friends were a year older. However, by the time I moved on to senior public school, I lost that group of companions as we were divided amongst various schools depending on where we lived. Once again, shyness kicked in as all of the students were at least a year older than me and the students were generally tougher and more street-wise than I was. Some of my friends had their first boyfriends at this time, but I was essentially afraid of boys. I didn't know how to act around them and didn't think that any of them would be interested in me. It wasn't until I was in grade eight that one of my teachers helped pull me out of my shell by encouraging my sense of humour and teaching me not to take life so seriously. His technique for accomplishing this was that he would put me into potentially embarrassing situations, then teach me to use my sense of humour to get out of them. Once, he stole one of my shoes and hid it, just at the opportune time when the bell rang signalling the students to switch classes. Instead, I simply removed the other shoe and went to Art barefoot. I thought he would be proud of me! Interestingly, this teacher was one of the major influences in my life at a time when family life was no picnic and when I didn't really have a social group that I was connected to at this school. However, I toughened up a bit during those years and by the time I graduated, I was ready to embrace highschool.

By grade nine, I realized that there were cool kids and uncool kids and I did not want to become part of the latter group. The cool kids were involved in sports and school government and I desperately wanted to be part of these. Fortunately, I was elected to student council every year and this helped myself-esteem considerably. The other component, I knew, was athletics and I knew that I was not a natural at team sports because of poor peripheral vision and lack of experience. Instead, I took up downhill skiing and tennis and did well at each. A new group of friends evolved at the location where I played tennis (even though it wasn't at school) and some of them became long-term companions.

By grade ten (age fourteen) my social skills were much better and I joined a sizeable group of peers that had a very positive and lasting effect on my life. We were all good students and all very involved in extracurricular activities such as sports or music. By this time, I was starting to develop the confidence to talk to boys although I was still very self-conscious. Fortunately, I became friends with two wonderful brothers who kept me laughing non-stop. On weekends, I began to go out dancing with friends and liked to dress like "cool kids". However, I was very unhappy that I didn't have a boyfriend at this time.

Then when I was fifteen, I had my first date. It was hell! I was so nervous and stupidly ordered spaghetti and salad at the restaurant (two foods that are very messy to eat). My mother had purchased a new yellow angora sweater for me to wear on my date and I proceeded to spill tomato sauce right down the front of it. I was devastated! Where was my much needed sense of humour then?

Finally, by grade thirteen, I met the older brother of one of my classmates. I'd had a crush on him for a couple of years before we actually met. He was absolutely zany and was six years older than me, and truly, I didn't know what I was doing, but I had somebody to go to the prom with and that was a big boost to my self-esteem. We were sort of a couple until I went away to university the next year.

First year science was difficult, unnerving and a bit lonely as I didn't have a social group once again. Underneath it all, I was still a shy person although by this time in my life, I had learned a few neat tricks to cover it up. Experience with a couple of short-term boyfriends helped, but I was really no expert on relationships with men, so I spent most of my time studying or hanging out with my roommate Glenda who was a great friend of mine from highschool. By my second year, I had a group and lived with them in an on-campus residence apartment. We were like one big, happy, crazy family and I remember the time as one of the best years in my life (probably because my own family life was so negative then). By my third year, I met my ex-husband, a socially immature man, which I didn't realize until I lived with him. It was during our short marriage of four years when I first experienced the symptoms of mental illness.

When I look back at my formative years and all the things that combined to form the person I am today, I sometimes wonder if I missed some developmental milestones along the way which affected my self-concept. I now ponder about whether there are any unique personality characteristics among those with bipolar disorder or whether my core personality has had an effect on the disorder or its outcome. Under the circumstances, does my personality help me or hurt me? Presently, I am content with the person I have become (warts and all) but I still have ups and downs like most people and I don't always recognize when I am being too hard on myself, or too easy.

Redfield- Jamison and Goodwin (2007, p. 325) suggest that an individual's temperament may have an effect on the outcomes of therapy and attitudes toward medication. Fortunately, my attitude towards medication is positive (I know that I need it and am committed to stay on it), so adherence is not a problem for me. Truly, some medications haven't worked or else have robbed me of my sense of self, but I never gave up. As a result, I have found the best treatment for me in terms of feeling quite "normal". In addition, I have always followed through with the psychotherapy that has been recommended for me. I now see a psychiatrist only once every two months to assess overall medication efficacy, sleep problems and level of overall wellness.

Patients' temperaments may affect the nature of their relationships with others, their ability to cope with stress and their tendency to develop problems with substance abuse. My relationships with others are now positive but during the most active phases of my illness, they certainly were not. When I was younger, I made poor decisions in terms of choosing men who would be potential life partners for me. I also experienced a lot of angry feelings towards my mother. Although I am divorced, time has passed , my judgment is much clearer now and I do not have any animosity toward others. As far as relationship quality is concerned, I am currently in the best place that I have ever been.

My ability to cope with stress is varied. Since I still have a debilitating sleep disorder, I don't always cope well with stress. I must continue to be vigilant about keeping negative stress to a minimum while maintaining enough positive pressure to stay motivated. I'm still working on this one.

Fortunately, I have never had an inclination towards substance abuse although some of my family members did. My father and my maternal grandmother battled alcohol addiction and as a result, I have always made a conscious effort not to follow in their footsteps. I certainly had a few carefree occasions in my youth when I drank socially, but I have never even experimented with illegal drugs or abused prescription medication. Luckily, I don't even like the taste of alcohol, nor can I afford the extra calories or the possible effects on medication so I choose not to drink and find that this behaviour involves no sacrifice. I do not foresee any problems with substance abuse in the future.

Recently, I have wondered whether or not medication affects my sense of identity or personality. I can recall feeling flat and sad during the period of time when I was undergoing lithium treatment. Although I was no longer hypomanic, I didn't feel quite myself, quite down and rather lethargic actually, and so I had to experiment with other medications. On my current medication, I feel like a normal person and others describe me as level-headed. Two medications, clomipramine and olanzapine help me maintain a stable sense of identity. I rarely struggle with crippling anxiety or with serious disruptions in mood. As a result, I have a pretty good idea of who I am. I remember the "old me" and feel closer to that personality than to the one I exhibited during the most acute phases of bipolar disorder. Some of my friends have said "It sucks to be normal", but I beg to differ.

Overall, it is difficult to draw conclusions about the effects of bipolar disorder on identity and visa versa, especially when medication is involved. Most research suggests that the personalities of bipolar patients are not fundamentally different from those of people without bipolar disorder. If anything about me has changed, it is for the better and this includes the effects of medication. Presently, I am content and I feel that I have a sense of self that is steadfast and enduring and I credit this state to working hard and being placed on an effective treatment regime.

The Creative Edge

Ah, I remember it well – the days when I could spin off yarns, invent one limerick after the other, engage in quick and ready banter or toy with marvellous puns – when ideas flowed like a rushing river, when I felt that I was at one with the universe. Everything seemed connected and somehow, everything made sense, at least to me. I developed theories about how ideas were generated and I had boundless energy. Writing pages and pages of theories about life, I found that my writing would inspire me even more. I would telephone my friends late at night to tell them about my discoveries and then I would jump in the car too charged to sit still and speed to my gym, work out for three hours then speed home (without getting caught). Sleep was impossible – the ideas just kept coming – theories about human thought, about the many wonderful careers I would have, and about how to influence the world with my capabilities. My creative energy was remarkable. I felt like I was on top of the world, in fact, in charge of the world!

Then all of a sudden – crash! Flashes of colour kept appearing before my eyes. The ideas all started running together and my responsibilities seemed overwhelming. I could not think straight. My head began to pound, as I became irritated, then enraged. Looking at all the material that I had written so furiously, it seemed that none of it made any sense at all. So I started to recite rhymes, but realized that they didn't make sense either. Furious with myself, I tried to slow down my mixed-up thoughts. But at one point, I thought I saw a secret code formed by titles of books on my bookshelves, so I telephoned my mother to tell her about it and to tell her that whatever I had, I was cured! She was alarmed. I wanted to live, but I wanted to die too. I was in trouble. So, what happened?

Mania, that's what. I can't live with it and I can't live without it or so I used to think. During the beginning stages of a manic episode, I would often be operating at peak performance, packing days of activity, reading and creating into one night. I often felt an incredible sense of well-being and began many projects. Mania or hypomania made me feel highly creative and everything had an urgency about it. But, this sensation didn't last, and I miss it, to a point. Honestly, I don't feel as creative now that I have recovered from the manic episodes of bipolar disorder, but I am learning to accept and manage the steadiness I now feel. I miss the highs and the good feelings but I am slowly learning how to access my creative side again with the addition of hard work and self-discipline. Some patients miss the high points too much and don't adhere to treatment. I do.

Socrates once said, "Madness, provided it comes with the gift of heaven, is the channel by which we receive the greatest blessings...the men of old who gave their names saw no disgrace or reproach in madness; otherwise, they would not have connected it with the name of the noblest of all arts, the art of discerning the future and called it the manic art" (Plato).

Many highly creative people in science, business and the arts are reluctant to accept treatment for bipolar disorder because they don't want to give up the creative edge they feel they get from it. These individuals see the variation in their moods as critical to their sense of self. Many of these people are concerned that psychiatric treatment will destroy their creative abilities and they see medication, in particular, as a hindrance.

However, is creativity clearly understood? Is it necessary to suffer in order to achieve great and creative accomplishments? Many might argue that intense emotion must accompany creativity – that it is associated with great imagination or magnificent works of art. In fact, creativity and excitement used to go hand in hand for me. It was during episodes of hypomania that I can recall feeling my most creative. And yet, looking back, I wonder whether I ever actually produced anything during those times. Was my creativity an illusion? What exactly is the nature of creativity anyway?

Creativity must include accomplishment – the perspiration as well as the inspiration. True, I was able to enjoy rhyming and word play during hypomanic phases and I started many projects, but was never able to complete them. In contrast to my previously distorted beliefs, creative achievement is, in essence a combination of intellectual ability, temperament, imagination, energy and hard work. It involves much discipline, devotion, time and flexibility. Creativity also involves the ability to generate a vast assortment of ideas, and to generate new, unusual and unique types of solutions. It requires divergent as opposed to convergent thinking.

There are a variety of personality characteristics associated with creativity. These include independence, energy, adaptability, persistence, self-confidence, risk-taking and insight. Creative people are often restless, enthusiastic and disinhibited as well. They must be open to information from the environment surrounding them and be able to put creative ideas into action. Creative accomplishnments require intense focus and often, long hours of work. According to Redfield- Jamison and

Goodwin (2007, p. 403), many creative people feel that inspiration and the creative act lead to a heightened mood, yet evidence suggests the opposite – that a state of euphoria precedes changes in thoughts and behaviour, and that intense creativity may be similar to hypomania.

Clearly, not all bipolar individuals are creative and not all creative people are bipolar. Hypomanic tendencies are only useful if accompanied by sustained attention, self-control and ability. It is important to note that many patients with bipolar disorder suffer from significant cognitive deficits as well as other symptoms while in the crux of mania.

How then could such an overwhelming illness be associated with great creative accomplishments? Many people believe that there may be a link. If there is, it is not necessarily a causal one. Perhaps the lifestyles of creative people lead to instability rather than visa versa. Perhaps expanded thoughts and emotions in hypomania could lead to the kind of ideas that precede creative achievement. Many successful achievers report changes in sleep and mood prior to deeply creative moments and describe creativity as a period of quicker, more fluid thinking, new ideas and novel connections (Redfield- Jamison, Goodwin, 2007, p. 398).

I have experienced this state of creativity and it has perhaps provided me with the motivation to write this book. However, I was not able to sustain attention and complete it until I was well again. In fact, my initial chapter notes, while unique, were somewhat bizarre and overly personalized. Yet results on the Wechsler Adult Intelligence Scale indicate that there may be higher intellectual functioning for individuals in a hypomanic state. In addition, similar personality characteristics exist in hypomanic and creative people (Redfield- Jamison, Goodwin, 2007, p.398).

But what about depression? It is part of the bipolar condition as well. Does it have an effect on creativity? When I was younger, I used to compose music when I was depressed. However, for the most part, I found that depression had a negative effect on my level of creativity although I know some bipolar artists who have said that their depressive experiences have been inspiring. These artists describe their paintings as dark, chaotic and filled with themes of death. During the depressive episodes I experienced, I know that I was not creative. Everything was slowed down and meaningless. I was unmotivated and uninspired. Occasionally, I would write during those times, but the content of my work tended to be redundant and self-absorbed. However, in a depressed mood, I have sometimes, (more practically perhaps), been able to edit previous work that was created in agitated chaos.

An important concern related to bipolar disorder and creativity has to do with medication. Some patients may feel cognitively or creatively stunted on some medications and may, as a result, refuse to take them. For these people, the cost of losing creativity outweighs the benefits of sanity. When I was first diagnosed with bipolar II disorder, this condition existed for me while I was on lithium, but by the time I was hospitalized for the second time, I had found a more suitable medication which has allowed me to function essentially at full capacity. However, everyone is different, and lithium certainly works for many people. In my opinion, this issue calls for a need to better research the effects of medication on creativity and productivity.

In conclusion, there is significant evidence connecting bipolar disorder to creativity but we don't yet know exactly what that connection is. It is interesting that both states are cyclic, and there are advantages and disadvantages to both. Some professions such as poetry and art may benefit more from mood changes than professions such as medicine which require constantly high levels of performance. Nevertheless, there is much literature available about the link between bipolar disorder and creativity. Biographies of many great individuals such as Van Gogh, Beethoven and Winston Churchill substantiate this although they cannot necessarily point to a cause-effect relationship. What is needed is ongoing investigation examining the processes in the brain that lead to cognitive changes occurring in hypomanic states.

PART THREE

CHAPTER 8
SURVIVE AND THRIVE

I'm out of the woods now, so to speak and I am fortunate since I know that many of my friends are still struggling. Following two ten-day stays in the hospital, I finally felt like my feet were back on the ground. Yet, I had a mess to sort out and I wouldn't be able to do it on my own. My finances were in shambles and my relationships with friends and family were in need of much repair. The icing on the cake was that I had been arrested for shoplifting during my last manic episode.

To me, money has either been friend or foe. Prior to my recovery, my track record with it had always been poor, especially over the last twenty years when I was symptomatic. Since 1988, I spent money and used credit without knowing how much I charged to my card or from where the money was coming to pay the bills. At the approximate time that my marriage ended, I certainly lost control and went on periodic and uninhibited shopping sprees. When I ran out of cash, I used my Visa card to get what I wanted. Over time, one credit card became five and I didn't even think about how I would pay this money back. My judgment was extremely impaired. I entertained such magical thoughts as, "the money will come from somewhere", or, "God will provide for me". However, a number of years ago, my purchases became more extravagant and I started to avoid paying any bills. Creditors would call and I promised to make payments – except I couldn't. I had a line of credit maxed out at $20,000, an overdraft of $1,500 and I had reached the limit on all of my credit cards. I couldn't even make the minimal interest payments each month. I had used the line of credit to pay for a trip to Africa which was terrible judgment on my part. My friend Cathy offered to help me pay back my debts by loaning me money at a lower interest rate but I was unable to follow through. The spending continued and regardless of what common sense others tried to instill in me, I was unreasonable and would not learn. Eventually, my mother bailed me out by paying Cathy back and by helping me with my other bills as well. However, I couln't follow rational advice and I had no impulse control. But, I didn't know why. Unsuccessfully, I even tried going to an addictions group and admitting that I was a shopaholic. Then, by the time I experienced my second round of hospitalization, in November, 2006, I had no money to pay my rent. Certain that my property management company would evict me if I was two weeks late, I did not know what to do. Upon discharge from the hospital, I was close to being destitute.

Once I was home, my recovery began with the help of a very resourceful crisis nurse who came to my home once every two weeks. We discussed my financial status, and she explained how my shopping behaviour had been part of my illness and not a separate addiction. She then communicated that she expected me to accept responsibility and to pay my debts now that I had been treated for bipolar disorder. I wondered how I would accomplish this. She indicated that I was in for a long, tough ride, but that I would now have a better chance at being successful and that I would likely be less impulsive. Truely, I was committed to change and follow through with the plan. The first thing this nurse taught me was that I could consolidate my debts by using a credit counselling service. I would pay a lower interest rate and pay a designated amount, without fail, every month. For some reason, I had never heard of an agency like this before and I was excited to get started and to get the situation under control. The nurse escorted me to the credit counsellor's office and guided me through the procedure. I would pay two hundred dollars per month for two and a half years and then I would be debt free at least as far as credit cards were concerned. Within the same stretch of time, I would also have to pay off nearly twenty other creditors. I can proudly say that I have achieved this goal and am debt free for the first time in over twenty years. At the beginning stages of this plan however, I was in a very different place. I did not have enough money to buy groceries and had to use a food bank for several months. These circumstances created severe stress for me. In order to save my home, I was required to write a letter to my property management company explaining how my mental illness had affected my financial behaviour and asking if I could pay double rent the following month. The company graciously allowed this and I have not missed a rent payment ever since.

Gradually, over the last few years, I have learned to manage my money better. There are still times when I enjoy shopping, but I can now look at nice things without having to buy them. I have learned to set goals and to save money for things I really need and for my future. Having a financial plan in the form of a written budget helps me to hold myself accountable and keeps me aware of how much money I have at any given time. If I am doubtful, I just look at the budget, do what it says and follow through. Things have become a lot easier for me now that I have recovered from bipolar symptoms.

In recovery, relationships matter – even if you live alone – especially if you live alone. My bizarre behaviour during my illness damaged (beyond repair in some cases) the relationships I had with family and friends. I frequently got angry with my mother and that wore us both out, and my negative feelings towards her were often enough to trigger a manic or depressive episode. In fact, until I responded to treatment, I felt that I had always had a strained relationship with my mother. Then somehow, when I got well, all that anger melted away. Perhaps, it was a kind of epiphany, but it seemed to happen in a moment and my mom and I have enjoyed a mutually supportive relationship ever since.

Some of my other relationships have literally vanished however. During the worst manic phases of my illness, my behaviour was peculiar and obnoxious. I often chose inappropriate people as friends, perhaps on impulse, to match the mood I was experiencing at the time. Where I had established good friendships I made some terrible mistakes, some of which I cannot recall to this day. Whatever they were, I have not been forgiven by some people and despite my effort to rekindle these relationships, I have not been successful in some cases. During my last manic episode I apparently (and I don't remember a thing about this), called friends or family late at night telling them that I had cancer, that there was a helicopter on the roof of my building waiting to take me to the United States and would they please wire me two thousand dollars to cover the cost. Fortunately, these unlucky people were eventually briefed about my condition by a knowledgeable family member or trusted friend. Yet despite my efforts to reach out and apologize, I have not heard from some of my friends ever since. Happily, I do have close friends and family who have supported me and been with me throughout my recovery. I have also met a number of new friends over the past few years and I am well able to use good judgment in choosing companions.

Getting caught by police for shoplifting was perhaps the biggest jolt in terms of convincing me that I was sick, although it wasn't until I had been in the hospital for a few days that I fully realized what had transpired in the grocery store, or was cognitively organized enough to deal with it. I was to go through a process called mental health diversion. A specialized officer of the court received documents from the hospital or therapist of the offender which substantiate the patient's level of illness during the offense. Once released from the hospital, I had an appointment with this officer at the courts, and she explained how the system works. I was expected to appear in court three times within the next year. After I did so, the charges were dropped (I haven't offended again) and a few months after that, my criminal records were destroyed by the police. Nevertheless, it was a harrowing and embarrassing experience, one that I never want to go through again.

With my finances and relationships on track and with my legal status cleared, I finally felt like it was time to take charge of my life in a more effective way. Managing life with mental illness requires a strong and positive attitude as well as a set of specialized skills for making improvements. Out with the old and in with the new.

One of the first things I had to learn was how to effectively advocate for myself. Fortunately, I am a resourceful person with a love of learning and even during active episodes of the illness, I knew that I needed to get help and I was persistent. I shudder to think about what would have happened to me if I had refused treatment and hospitalization. I might have ended up in jail! Even though I have been free of symptoms for almost four years, I still read a great deal about bipolar disorder and am learning to commumicate my needs to others. Education truly is one of the best forms of treatment. I want to know how to get well and stay well.

Self advocacy improves self-esteem and forces you to organize your life in such a way that you can be independent. Even when I was very ill and had to consider power of attorney for my care and finances, I knew, deep down, that I had to learn to take care of myself and be independent, as I live alone. I knew that unless I tested my ability to manage money, relationships and lifestyle, I would never really know if I could do these things on my own. Therefore, even though I was a step away from ruin, I knew that, with help, I had to solve my own problems. It takes effort to stand up for yourself, but it is worth it and it is necessary.

Mental health patients need to do several things in order to advocate effectively for themselves. Firstly, patients need to educate themselves about bipolar disorder through reading, discussing issues with clinicians and through writing down important information. It is also wise to keep a file of this information and to update it regularly. Secondly, patients must know their rights and must know under what conditions they would allow others to make decisions for them. For example, I have arranged for a good friend of mine to have power of attorney for care and finances should I become too ill to manage these responsibilities. I do not expect this situation to arise because I am committed to my treatment program but I feel that this arrangement is necessary to be safe and proactive. Thirdly, bipolar patients must know their needs and be able to communicate them clearly to others. This should be done when the patient is well enough to be organized, accurate and assertive. For example, I decided that I needed a new place to live that was private, quiet and conveniently located since I do not have a car. A few years ago, I was renting a loft apartment in a house, but had to share a kitchen. In addition, I found the landlady intrusive, loud and emotionally unstable. As my illness progressed, I found this living arrangement highly stressful. Now, I have a spacious, quiet apartment that is centrally located, near a shopping plaza and close to public transit. Although it is expensive, I have peace of mind here and I can now manage it financially. Finally in order to self-advocate, it is important for patients to develop a written treatment plan for themselves which includes information about medication, doctors, power of attorney and any treatment issues their family or friends should know about. Although it may seem premature, a will should be drafted and assigned to an executor. Development of a treatment plan should take place when the patient is well and even though he or she may never need it, the steps are in place in case they do. Treatment plan documents should include a list of symptoms the patient might be experiencing, the names of people who have the power to make decisions on her behalf, medications and dosages, medications to avoid (due to allergies or known side-effeccts), preferred hospital location, a list of doctors and other health care providers, a list of contacts (friends, family and legal) and any specific instructions people would need to follow.

An important component of wellness in any treatment plan but especially in one for bipolar disorder includes a strong support system. I cannot emphasize this enough. When my bipolar symptoms began to worsen, I initially denied the disorder or at least tried to hide it. As a result, I alienated people at a time when I really needed them to understand me and act on my behalf. Therefore, even when I was in psychosis, it took me a full week of trips to the emergency ward in order to be admitted for psychiatric treatment. Each day I went (until the last), I was alone, without support and found it nearly impossible to stand up for myself. If I had been left alone any longer, I may have become suicidal.

Fortunately, I was eventually hospitalized on a day where I did have someone with me and after about five days on medication, I was lucid enough to start building and organizing a stable support network. It is critically important to have others monitor how you are doing when you have bipolar disorder as it is difficult to assess when you are manic in this illness. Also, others can advocate for you when you are in need of treatment. At a time when you are well, educate the members of your support team so that they know exactly what you need in case of a relapse, and provide for them the names and numbers of physicians involved in your case. Other patients may become members of your support team as well if you are attending a facilitated support group for bipolar patients. I met a good friend of mine through a group and he regularly gives me feedback on how I am doing.

It is important to note that the relationship between you and your support team is reciprocal. There may be times when these people will need you. So, do what you can to stay well and stay in touch with the people who are important to you, and keep broadening your support network so you aren't leaning too heavily on any one person.

Armed with a strong support group, a number of medical and psychiatric experts and medication which virtually eliminated my bipolar symptoms, I was ready to choose a healthy lifestyle and make positive choices for myself. As a bipolar patient, I had to learn how to structure my life in order to minimize stress while at the same time challenge myself to try new things. Since I have been treated with medication, most of my symptoms have dissipated except for a troubling sleep disorder. While working as a teacher, this condition became highly problematic as I would often either fall asleep in class or miss work due to cumulative sleep loss. I therefore had to be placed on long term disability so that I could be flexible if I needed to catch up on sleep. This sleep disorder is chronic and has been with me for many years, but for some reason, despite attempting good sleep hygiene, it continues to get worse. I have tried nearly every sleep medication and sedative on the market but I simply do not respond to them. Nevertheless, I have tried to structure my days to include exercise, writing, visiting friends and family, taking care of my home and reading. It is a simple lifestyle but it keeps me from becoming overwhelmed by a schedule I can no longer manage.

Exercise is critical for me, especially since my medication contributes to weight gain. I work out five days a week and walk for an hour on off days. I try to avoid candy, sugar and fried foods as much as possible and try to eat more protein, vegetables and fruit. I have lost some weight and I will not give up but I have not reached my goal for weight loss yet. However, I will not give up. Feeling good involves exercising and eating well and I do my best to stay on track.

Writing has been therapeutic for me for a number of reasons. Firstly, by establishing a writing time each day (duration of two to four hours), I create structure and purpose in my life. Secondly, writing requires discipline and focus, and the more I do it, the easier it gets. When this book is finished, I have an idea for another one. Writing has been beneficial for me for many other reasons as well. Firstly, this project has forced me to conduct research on bipolar disorder and has increased my knowledge about the disorder tenfold. Secondly, it has improved my ability to be cognitively organized. This is important to me because I have experienced some cognitive dulling while on my medication. Thirdly, writing requires sustained attention and has helped me move from impulsivity to more reflective behaviours. Finally, when it is completed, I hope that this book will be a useful tool for others to read in familiarizing themselves with bipolar disorder.

I have, over the years, become an independent person, sometimes to such a degree that I neglect to include others in my life because I am used to being alone. In my mid twenties, I was married for a short time, but since then, I have been single and have become more self-reliant. In addition, I am a voracious reader and I relish the times I have with good books. However, I now know that in order to be healthy, I must schedule some social time into most days or risk being lonely. Fortunately, I have good friends and supportive family members to spend time with. It is still a goal of mine to establish a broader social circle and I am currently looking at new ways of doing this. However, as long as I see a few people each week, I feel content.

One aspect of my life that is very important to me is my home. I have a flair for interior design and like to create spaces that reflect who I am and what I like. My apartment is modern, spacious and bright, and I have enjoyed displaying my collections of African art, tropical plants and books. Slowly but surely, I am getting rid of things I don't need such as clothing and household items. My space is full but organized, clean and neat. Large windows and bright lights allow me to keep my home well lit, which I need, since I find that my mood is better if I am surrounded by light. The depth of winter can be a challenge for me, so I tend to keep bright lights on when I am home. My apartment is also in an ideal location for me, in north central Toronto with easy access to local transit and a shopping plaza. The building is quiet with lots of green spaces surrounding it, an outdoor pool and a park across the street. It is my cocoon.

Overall, there have been numerous important tasks to attend to in order for me to recover from my episodes of bipolar disorder. I've had to learn how to manage money, improve the quality of my relationships and deal with legal issues. The tools of self advocacy have made me aware of my needs and the communication of them to others. My support network continues to grow and I have a new sense of purpose in my life. Very importantly, my recovery has been directed by me and I have chosen to focus on my strengths as opposed to my weaknesses. Finally, I have given back. I volunteer at the hospital that treated me and this experience forces me to take the focus off myself and to take care of others.

For four years, thanks to medication and therapy, I have been well. However, personal growth for anyone takes effort, responsibility, compassion and wisdom. I have emerged from this illness with humility, hope and reverence for those who have fought a similar battle. I have been moved by the extraordinary stories of others I've met along the way, their joys and sorrows and their accomplishments. Recovery is a life-long journey for individuals with bipolar disorder and I hope that readers will find this book to be a valuable tool along their own roads to wellness.

AFTERWORD

It is December 8, 2006. I have been discharged and have come home. Opening the door slowly, I take in my surroundings as if I were entering a brand new world. In some ways, I suppose I am. In many ways, I feel like a new person in that I have been given a second chance to make things right.

Gingerly, I step into the apartment – quiet, peaceful and welcoming – and allow the space to embrace me. There is no rush to turn on the television or stereo for company – I am comfortable with the silence and the aloneness. Little things like the coo of a dove on the balcony or the sight of my Christmas tree beckon me to enter. Quietly, I take a stroll through each room and notice that everything is in its place. I feel no need to call everyone and let them know I am home, and in fact, I choose to wait a day before contacting people. The last two weeks have been spent sharing life space with twenty-five other psychiatric patients and I now desperately want the quiet. I decide to test myself to make sure that I will still be comfortable living alone.

Initially, even though I am glad to be back in my apartment, I am somewhat unsettled, absent-minded and distractible. In the first few days, I do things like leaving a burner on with an egg boiling on top (the fire department are called when I am out), I pour orange juice all over the floor thinking that I have set a glass out and I find my flashlight in the laundry hamper. For some reason, I also forget most phone numbers that I have previously committed to memory, including my own and those of family members. Accidently, I break glasses and dishes and realize that I must endeavour to move slowly until I get my concentration back.

The first couple of nights of sleeping at home are very odd. I fall asleep before midnight but wake every two or three hours soaked with sweat. I shower, change the sheets and it happens again. At six a.m. each morning, I bounce out of bed thinking that I have missed the day. This may be residual mania or adjustment to new medication. But alas, on the third night, I have my usual dose of insomnia and wake up tired the next day.

Nevertheless, my recovery is rapid and I now think about how different my life will be. Familiarity with bipolar disorder and its treatment allow me to put things in place to make sure that I never (hopefully) have a relapse of depression or mania again. In rebuilding my life I am now free to explore possibilities that a normal person would investigate. I can write a book, exercise at the gym, manage my finances, spend time with family and friends, travel, volunteer, read, learn and grow.

I do wonder how I will be doing in a few years. Will I ever regain the memories lost during the crux of my illness? Will I ever be able to sleep normally? Will I be upset that I cannot work at a regular job anymore or that I cannot achieve some of the goals I set during wild states of hypomania or mania? Will I ever suffer a relapse?

One thing I do have is hope, for wellness and for a bright future. I have dreams, aspirations and goals. Madness is no longer such a huge part of my life. But, the study of the mind is. I have always been and continue to be fascinated by the brain's structure, function and scope and the more I learn about it, the more I realize how much there is yet to uncover. Having bipolar disorder these past years has taught me about how powerful and yet delicate is the mind.

Although I have experienced a great deal of relief from the unbearable symptoms of bipolar disorder, it has been the imperfect parts of the mind that have drawn me to its study and to a career working with troubled youth and children. While I have worked hard to develop the positive aspects of myself, it is the dark side that still interests me. Both sides of mind define me and although I would have enjoyed a life free of bipolar symptoms, I also would have missed the opportunity to know and understand such a great variety of people with unique and extraordinary minds and lives. The years of living with bipolar disorder have made me more thoughtful, empathic, curious, courageous and resilient. These years have in fact given me a sense of purpose and a wish to communicate it through this book and my work with others. And so, I now invite you as the reader to embark on your own journey and experiences while exploring, as you go, the other side of mind.

Bibliography

1. Burgess, W.,*The Bipolar Handbook*, Penguin Group, New York, 2006
2. *Canadian Mental Health Association*, 2160 Yonge Street, Third floor, Toronto, Ontario, M4S 2Z3, 416-484-7750, www.cmha.ca
3. Castle, L., R., *Finding Your Bipolar Muse.* Marlowe and Company, New York, 2006
4. *Centre for Addiction and Mental Health Information Centre.* 33 Russell Street, Toronto, Ontario, M5S 2S1, 416-595-6111, Toll-free 1-800-463-6273, www.camh.net
5. Copeland, M. E., *Living with Depression and Manic Depression.* New Harbinger Publications, Inc., Oakland, California
6. *Desk Reference to the Diagnostic Criteria from DSM IV.* American Psychiatric Association, Washington D.C., 1994
7. Duke, M., Nowicki, S., *Abnormal Psychology.* Wadsworth Publishing Company Inc., California, 1979

8. Edwards, V. *Depression and Bipolar Disorders.* Key Porter Books, Toronto, Ontario, 2002

9. Fieve, R.R., *Moodswing.* Bantom Books, Toronto, 1997

10. First, M.B., Frances, A., Pincus, H. A., *DSM IV TR Guidebook.* American Psychiatric Publishing, Inc., Washington D.C., 2004

11. Frank, E., *Treating Bipolar Disorder.* The Guilford Press, New York, 2005

12. Goodwin, F.K., Redfield Jamison, K., *Manic Depressive Illness.* Oxford University Press, U.S.A., 2007

13. Hornbacher, M., *Madness – A Bipolar Life* Houghton Mifflin Company, New York, 2008

14. Jamison, K., R., *Touched with Fire.* Freepress Paperbacks, New York, 1993

15. Jamison, K., R., *An Unquiet Mind.* Vintage Books, New York, 1995

16. Lickey, M. E., Gordon, B., *Medicine and Mental Illness.* W.H. Freeman and Company, U.S.A., 1991

17. Miklowitz, D. J., *The Bipolar Survival Guide.* The Guilford Press, New York, 2002

18. Mondimore, F.M. *Bipolar Disorder.* The John Hopkins University Press, Baltimore, 1999

19. *Mood Disorders Association of Ontario and Toronto.* 40 Orchard View Blvd., Suite 222, Toronto, Ontario, M4R 1B9

20. Papolos, D., Papolos, J.,*The Bipolar Child.* Broadway Books, New York, 2006

21. Suppes, T., Sloan Manning, J., Keck, P. E., *Decoding Bipolar Disorder*. Compact Clinicals, Kansas City, 2007
22. Torrey, E. F., Knable, D. O., *Surviving Manic Depression*. Basic Books, U.S.A., 2005

ABOUT THE AUTHOR

A native of Toronto, Sarah Smyth is a teacher and family counsellor with Special Education qualifications in behavioural and psychiatric disorders, learning disabilities and giftedness. She has thirty years of experience helping children and adults with developmental and psychiatric needs.